HOPE

IN TIMES OF TROUBLE

Seeking Answers In Life's Struggles

DISCOVERY HOUSE

PUBLISHERS®

Contents

PREFACE

The ancient book of Job reminds us of one of life's greatest realities, "Man who is born of woman is of few days and full of trouble" (Job 14:1). We are surrounded by events and struggles that are beyond us, that are too big for us. In the midst of those challenges, it is valuable to know that the God of heaven knows and understands the burdens of life in a fallen world. He cares and is involved and His love for us is undiminished by the hardnesses of life.

To help us see the great heart of God's care during life's struggles, we have collected teaching from RBC Ministries' Discovery Series to point us to Him. We trust that this volume will help us to find *Hope In Times of Trouble*.

ONE

Why Would A Good God Allow Suffering?

I t's an old question. Four thousand years ago, a victim of personal, family, and financial reversals spoke to the silent heavens and pleaded, "Show me why You contend with me. Does it seem good to You that You should oppress, that You should despise the work of Your hands?" (Job 10:2-3). The questions are still being asked. "Does God hate me? Is this why He is allowing me to suffer like this? Why me and not others?"

There are answers. Not exhaustive, but enough to keep our pain in perspective. Enough to show us how to put suffering to work for us. In the following pages, Kurt De Haan, who was managing editor for *Our Daily Bread* until his death in 2003, shows us that while heaven may not be answering all our questions, it is giving us all the answers we need to trust and love the One who, in our pain, is calling us to Himself.

MARTIN R. DE HAAN II

Elusive Answers

Life can be hard to understand. In trying to come to grips with the cold realities of our existence, we can easily become frustrated. We long for answers to the immense problem of suffering. We may even wonder if we will ever fully comprehend why bad things happen to good people and why good things happen to bad people. The answers often seem to be elusive, hidden, out-of-reach.

Oh, it makes sense that a terrorist would be killed by his own bomb. It makes sense that a reckless driver would be in a serious accident. It makes sense that a person who plays with fire would get burned. It even makes sense that a chain-smoker would develop lung cancer.

But what about the innocent men, women, and children who are killed by a terrorist's bomb? What about the young driver who suffers severe brain damage because a drunk veered over the center line? What about the person whose home burns down due to no fault of his own? And what about the 2-year-old child with leukemia?

It is dangerous, even foolish, to pretend that we have a complete answer as to why God allows suffering. The reasons are many and complex. It's just as wrong to demand that we *should* understand. Old Testament sufferer Job realized that he had no right to demand an answer from God, saying, "Therefore I have uttered what I did not understand, things too wonderful for me, which I did not know" (Job 42:3).

But God *has* given us some answers. Although we may not be able to know why one person gets singled out for a disease, we can know part of the reason diseases exist. And even though we may not understand why we face a certain problem, we can know how to deal with the situation and respond in a way that pleases the Lord.

> *"The fact of suffering undoubtedly constitutes the single greatest challenge to the Christian faith."*
>
> —John Stott

One more thing. I am not going to pretend that I fully understand the suffering that you may be experiencing. Although some aspects of human pain are common, the particulars are different. And what you may need most right now is not a four-point outline on why you are suffering or even what to do about it. What you may need most is a hug, a listening ear, or someone who will just sit with you in silence. Sometime along the way, however, you will want and need biblical truth to comfort you and help you to see your plight from God's perspective.

You and I need more than untested theories. That's why I have tried to include the insights of people who have suffered a variety of physical and emotional pains. My prayer for you is that your faith in God will stand firm even when your world seems to be falling apart.

Why Would A Good God Allow Suffering?

In our world of pain, where is God? If He is good and compassionate, why is life often so tragic? Has He lost control? Or, if He is in control, what is He trying to do to me and to others?

Some people have chosen to deny God's existence because they cannot imagine a God who would allow such misery. Some believe that God exists, but they want nothing to do with Him because they don't think He could be good. Others have settled for a belief in a kindly God who loves us but has lost control of a rebellious planet. Still others cling tenaciously to a belief in an all-wise, all-powerful, loving God who somehow uses evil for good.

As we search the Bible, we discover that it paints a picture of a God who can do anything He chooses to do. Sometimes He has acted in mercy and performed miracles in behalf of His people. At other times, though, He has chosen to do nothing to stop tragedy. He is supposed to be intimately involved in our lives, yet at times He seems deaf to our cries for help. In the Bible, He assures us that He controls all that happens, but He sometimes lets us be the targets of evil people, bad genes, dangerous viruses, or natural disasters.

If you're like me, you long for some way to put together an answer to this puzzling issue of suffering. I believe that God has given us enough pieces of the puzzle to help us trust Him even when we don't have all the information we would like. In this brief study we will see that the basic answers of the Bible are that our good God allows pain and suffering in our world to alert us to the problem of sin, to direct us to respond to Him in faith and hope, to shape us to be more like Christ, and to unite us so that we will help each other.

TO ALERT US

Imagine a world without pain. What would it be like? At first the idea may sound appealing. No more headaches. No more backaches. No more upset stomachs. No more throbbing sensations when the hammer misses the mark and lands on your thumb. No more sore throats. But there would also be no more sensation to alert you of a broken bone or tearing ligaments. No alarm to let you know that an ulcer is eating a hole in your stomach. No discomfort to warn of a cancerous tumor that is gathering forces for a takeover of your body. No angina to let you know that the blood vessels to your heart are clogging up. No pain to signal a ruptured appendix.

As much as we may abhor pain, we have to admit that it often serves a good purpose. It warns us when something goes wrong. The cause of the misery, rather than the agony itself, is the real problem. Pain is merely a symptom, a siren or bell that sounds when a part of the body is endangered or under attack.

In this section we will see how pain could be God's way to alert us that:

1. Something's wrong with the world.
2. Something's wrong with God's creatures.
3. Something's wrong with me.

Any one of these problems could be the reason for the pain in our lives. Let's look at each possible diagnosis.

1. Something's Wrong With The World.

The sorry condition of our planet indicates that something has gone terribly wrong. The suffering we experience and the distress we sense in others indicate that suffering does not discriminate on the basis of race, social status, religion, or even morality. It can seem cruel, random, purposeless, grotesque, and wildly out of control. Bad things happen to people who try to be good, and good things happen to people who enjoy being bad.

The seeming unfairness of it all has struck close to each of us. I remember watching my grandmother as she was dying of cancer. Grandma and Grandpa Blohm moved in with our family. My mother, a registered nurse, took care of her during her final months. Mom administered the pain killer. Grandpa desperately wanted her to be healed. Then the day came when the hearse pulled up and took away her frail, wasted body. I knew she was in heaven, but it still hurt. I hated cancer—I still do.

As I sit here thinking of all the suffering that my friends, co-workers, family, neighbors, and church family have experienced, I can hardly believe the length of the list—and my list is incomplete. So often these people have suffered through no apparent fault of their own. An accident, a birth defect, a genetic disorder, a miscarriage, an abusive parent, chronic pain, a rebellious child, a severe illness, random disease, the death of a spouse or a child, a broken relationship, a natural disaster. It just doesn't seem fair. From time to time I'm tempted to give in to frustration.

How do we resolve this? How do we live with the cold facts of life without denying reality or being overcome with despair? Couldn't God have created a world where nothing would ever go wrong? Couldn't He have made a world where people would never have the ability to make a bad choice or ever hurt another person? Couldn't He have made a world where mosquitos, weeds, and cancer would never exist? He could have—but He didn't.

The great gift of human freedom that He has given to us, the ability to choose, carries with it the risk of making wrong choices.

If you could choose between being a free-thinking creature in a world where bad choices produce suffering or being a robot in a world without pain, what would you decide? What kind of being would bring more honor to God? What kind of creature would love Him more?

We could have been created to be like the cute battery-operated dolls that say, "I love you" when hugged. But God had other plans. He took a "risk" to create beings who could do the unthinkable—rebel against their Creator.

What happened in paradise? Temptation, bad choices, and tragic consequences destroyed the tranquility of Adam and Eve's existence. Genesis 2 and 3 detail how Satan tested their love for the Lord—and they failed. In biblical terms, that failure is called sin. And just as the AIDS virus infects a body, breaks down the body's immune system, and leads to death, so also sin spreads as a deadly infection that passes from one generation to the next. Each new generation inherits the effects of sin and the desire to sin (Rom. 1:18-32; 5:12,15,18).

> "The Bible traces the entrance of suffering and evil into the world to a grand but terrible quality of human beings—freedom."
>
> –Philip Yancey

Not only did the entrance of sin into the world have devastating effects on the nature of human beings, but sin also brought about immediate and continual judgment from God. Genesis 3 relates how physical and spiritual death became a part of human existence (vv.3,19), childbirth became painful (v.16), the ground was cursed with weeds that would make man's work very difficult (vv.17-19), and Adam and Eve were evicted from the special Garden where they had enjoyed intimate fellowship with God (vv.23-24).

In the New Testament, the apostle Paul described the whole creation of God as groaning and eagerly anticipating the time when it will be freed from the curse of decay and be remade, free from the effects of sin (Rom. 8:19-22).

Disease, disaster, and corruption are symptoms of a deeper problem—the human race has rebelled against the Creator. Every sorrow, grief, and agony is a vivid reminder of our human predicament. Like a huge neon sign, the reality of suffering screams the message that the world is not the way God created it to be.

Therefore, the first and most basic answer to the problem of the existence of suffering is that it is the direct result of sin's entrance into the world. Pain alerts us that a spiritual disease is wracking our planet. Many times our troubles may be merely the side-effects of living in a fallen world—through no direct fault of our own.

2. Something's Wrong With God's Creatures.

We can be targets of cruel acts from other people or from Satan's rebel army. Both fallen human beings and fallen spirit beings (angels who have rebelled) have the capacity to make decisions that damage themselves and others.

Suffering can be caused by people. As free (and sin-infected) creatures, people have made and will continue to make many bad choices in life. These bad choices often affect other people.

For example, one of Adam's sons, Cain, made a choice to kill his brother Abel (Gen. 4:7-8). Lamech boasted about his violence (vv.23-24). Sarai mistreated Hagar (Gen. 16:1-6). Laban swindled his nephew Jacob (Gen. 29:15-30). Joseph's brothers sold him into slavery (Gen. 37:12-36), and then Potiphar's wife falsely accused him of attempted rape and had him thrown into prison (Gen. 39). Pharaoh cruelly mistreated the Jewish slaves in Egypt (Ex. 1). King Herod slaughtered all the babies who lived in and around Bethlehem in an attempt to kill Jesus (Mt. 2:16-18).

> *"God whispers to us in our pleasures, speaks in our conscience, but shouts in our pain; it is His megaphone to rouse a deaf world."*
> —C. S. Lewis

The hurt that others inflict on us may be due to selfishness on their part. Or we may be the target of persecution because of our faith in Christ. Throughout history, people who have identified with the Lord have suffered at the hands of those who rebelled against God.

Before his conversion, Saul was a rabid anti-Christian who did all he could to make life miserable for believers—even working to have them put to death (Acts 7:54–8:3). But after his dramatic turn to the Lord Jesus, he bravely endured all types of persecution as he boldly proclaimed the gospel message

(2 Cor. 4:7-12; 6:1-10). He could even say that the suffering he endured helped to make him more like Christ (Phil. 3:10).

Suffering can also be caused by Satan and demons. Job's life story is a vivid example of how a good person can suffer incredible tragedy because of satanic attack. God allowed Satan to take away Job's possessions, his family, and his health (Job 1–2).

I cringed even as I wrote the preceding sentence. Somehow, and for His reasons, God allowed Satan to devastate Job's life. We may tend to compare this to a father who allows the neighborhood bully to beat up his children just to see if they would still love Dad afterward. But, as Job came to realize, that's not a fair assessment when speaking about our wise and loving God.

We know, though Job did not, that his life was a test case, a living testimonial to the trustworthiness of God. Job illustrated that a person can trust God and maintain integrity even when life falls apart (for whatever reason), because God is worth trusting. In the end, Job learned that even though he didn't understand what God was up to, he had plenty of reason to believe that God was not being unjust, cruel, sadistic, or unfair by allowing his life to be ripped apart (Job 42).

The apostle Paul experienced a physical problem that he attributed to Satan. He called it a "thorn in the flesh . . . , a messenger of Satan to buffet me" (2 Cor. 12:7). Paul prayed to be freed from the problem, but

God didn't give him what he asked for. Instead, the Lord helped him to see how this difficulty could serve a good purpose. It made Paul humbly dependent on the Lord and put him in a position to experience His grace (vv.8-10).

Although most cases of sickness cannot be directly tied to Satan's work, the gospel accounts do record a few examples of suffering attributed to Satan, including a blind and mute man (Mt. 12:22) and a boy who suffered seizures (17:14-18).

3. Something's Wrong With Me.

Too often when something goes wrong in our lives we immediately jump to the conclusion that God is whipping us because of some sin we've committed. That's not necessarily true. As I indicated in the previous points, much of the suffering that comes into our lives is because we live in a broken world inhabited by broken people and rebellious spirit beings.

Job's friends mistakenly thought that he was suffering because of sin in his life (Job 4:7-8; 8:1-6; 22:4-5; 36:17). Jesus' own disciples jumped to the wrong conclusion when they saw a blind man. They wondered if the man's sight problem was due to his personal sin or because of something his parents had done (Jn. 9:1-2). Jesus told them that the man's physical problem was not related to his personal sin or the sin of his parents (v.3).

With these cautions in mind, we need to deal with the hard truth that some suffering does come as the direct consequence of sin—either as corrective discipline from God for those He loves, or punitive action by God upon rebels in His universe.

Correction. If you and I have placed our trust in Jesus Christ as our Savior, we are children of God. As such, we are

part of a family headed by a loving Father who trains and corrects us. He's not an abusive, sadistic parent who dishes out severe beatings because He gets some twisted pleasure out of it.

Hebrews 12 states:

> My son, do not despise the chastening of the Lord, nor be discouraged when you are rebuked by Him; for whom the Lord loves He chastens, and scourges every son whom He receives. . . . Furthermore, we have had human fathers who corrected us, and we paid them respect. Shall we not much more readily be in subjection to the Father of spirits and live? For they indeed for a few days chastened us as seemed best to them, but He for our profit, that we may be partakers of His holiness (vv. 5-6, 9-10).

And to the church in Laodicea, Jesus said, "As many as I love, I rebuke and chasten. Therefore be zealous and repent" (Rev. 3:19).

King David knew what it was like to experience the tough love of the Lord. After his adultery with Bathsheba and his conniving to ensure that her husband would be killed in battle, David did not repent until the prophet Nathan confronted him. Psalm 51 recounts David's struggle with guilt and his cry for forgiveness. In another psalm, David reflected on the effects of covering up and ignoring sin. He wrote, "When I kept silent, my bones grew old through my groaning all the day long. For day and night Your hand was heavy upon me" (Ps. 32:3-4).

In 1 Corinthians 11:27-32, the apostle Paul warned believers that treating the things of the Lord lightly—partaking of the Lord's Supper without taking it seriously—will bring discipline. Paul explained that this discipline of the Lord was purposeful. He said, "When we are judged, we are chastened by the Lord, that we may not be condemned with the world" (v. 32).

Most of us can understand the principle that whom God loves He disciplines. We would expect a loving Father to correct us and call us to renew our obedience to Him.

Judgment. God also acts to deal with stubborn unbelievers who persist in doing evil. A person who has not received God's gift of salvation can expect to receive God's wrath at a future day of judgment and faces the danger of harsh judgment now if God so chooses.

The Lord brought the flood to destroy decadent humanity (Gen. 6). He destroyed Sodom and Gomorrah (Gen. 18–19). He sent plagues on the Egyptians (Ex. 7–12). He commanded Israel to completely destroy the pagans who inhabited the

Promised Land (Dt. 7:1-3). He struck down the arrogant King Herod of New Testament times (Acts 12:19-23). And at the future day of judgment, God will deal out perfect justice to all those who reject His love and rule (2 Pet. 2:4-9).

In the here-and-now, however, we face inequities. For His all-wise reasons, God has chosen to delay His perfect justice. The psalm writer Asaph struggled with this apparent unfairness of life. He wrote about the wicked who were getting away with their evil deeds, even prospering, while many of the righteous were having

> *"My son, do not despise the chastening of the Lord, nor be discouraged when you are rebuked by Him; for whom the Lord loves He chastens."*
>
> —HEBREWS 12:5-6

troubles (Ps. 73). Concerning the prosperity of the wicked he said, "When I thought how to understand this, it was too painful for me—until I went into the sanctuary of God; then I understood their end" (vv.16-17). By thinking of the sovereign Lord of the universe, Asaph was able to get things back into perspective.

When we struggle with the reality that wicked people are literally "getting away with murder" and all sorts of immorality, we need to remember that "the Lord is . . . longsuffering toward us, not willing that any should perish but that all should come to repentance" (2 Pet. 3:9).

The first part of the answer, then, to the problem of suffering is that God uses it to alert us to serious problems. Pain sounds the alarm that indicates something is wrong with the world, with humanity at large, and with you and me. But as we will see in the next section, God not only signals the problems but He also uses troubles to encourage us to find the solutions—in Him.

TO DIRECT US

When a person turns away from God, suffering often gets the blame. But strangely, suffering also gets the credit when people describe what redirected their lives, helped them to see life more clearly, and caused their relationship with God to grow closer. How can similar circumstances have such radically different effects on people? The reasons lie deep within the people, not the events.

A well-known and outspoken media leader publicly denounced Christianity as "a religion for losers." But he has not always felt that way. As a young man he had Bible training, including a Christian prep school. When joking about the heavy indoctrination he received, he said, "I think I was saved seven or eight times." But then a painful experience changed his outlook on life and God. His younger sister became very ill. He prayed for her healing, but after 5 years of suffering she died. He became disillusioned with a God who would allow that to happen. He said, "I began to lose my faith, and the more I lost it the better I felt."

What makes the difference between someone like him and a person like Joni Eareckson Tada? In *Where Is God When It Hurts?* Philip Yancey describes the gradual transformation that took place in Joni's attitude in the years after she was paralyzed in a diving accident.

"At first, Joni found it impossible to reconcile her condition with her belief in a loving God. . . . The turning to God was very gradual. A melting in her attitude from bitterness to trust dragged out over three years of tears and violent questioning" (pp. 133-34).

A turning point came the evening that a close friend, Cindy, told her, "Joni, you aren't the only one. Jesus knows how you feel—why, He was paralyzed too." Cindy described how Jesus was fastened to the cross, paralyzed by the nails.

Yancey then observed, "The thought intrigued Joni and, for a moment, took her mind off her own pain. It had never occurred to her that God might have felt the same piercing sensations that now racked her body. The realization was profoundly comforting" (p.134).

Instead of continuing to search for why the devastating accident occurred, Joni has been forced to depend more heavily on the Lord and to look at life from a long-range perspective.

Yancey further says about Joni, "She wrestled with God, yes, but she did not turn away from Him. . . . Joni now calls her accident a 'glorious intruder,' and claims it was the best thing that ever happened to her.

God used it to get her attention and direct her thoughts toward Him" (pp. 137-38).

This principle that suffering can produce healthy dependence on God is taught by the apostle Paul in one of his letters to the church in Corinth. He wrote:

We do not want you to be ignorant, brethren, of our trouble which came to us in Asia: that we were burdened beyond measure, above strength, so that we despaired even of life. Yes, we had the sentence of death in ourselves, that we should not trust in ourselves but in God who raises the dead (2 Cor. 1:8-9).

A similar idea can be found in Paul's comments about his physical troubles. The Lord told Paul, "My grace is sufficient for you, for My strength is made perfect in weakness" (2 Cor. 12:9). Then Paul added, "Therefore I take pleasure in infirmities, in reproaches, in needs, in persecutions, in distresses, for Christ's sake. For when I am weak, then I am strong" (v.10).

Suffering has a way of showing how limited and weak our own resources really are. It forces us to rethink priorities, values, goals, dreams, pleasures, the source of real strength, and our relationships with people and with God. It has a way of directing our attention to spiritual realities—if we don't turn from God instead.

Suffering forces us to evaluate the direction of our lives. We can choose to despair by focusing on our present problems, or we can choose to hope by recognizing God's long-range plan for us (Rom. 5:5; 8:18-28; Heb. 11).

Of all the passages in the Bible, Hebrews 11 most reassures me that whether life is grand or grotesque, my response needs to be one of faith in the wisdom, power, and control of God. No matter what, I have good reason to trust Him—just as the great men and women of old hoped in Him.

For example, Hebrews 11 reminds us about Noah, a man who spent 120 years waiting for God to fulfill His promise of a devastating flood (Gen. 6:3). Abraham waited many agonizing years before the child whom God had promised was finally born. Joseph was sold into slavery and wrongfully imprisoned, but he finally saw how God used all the apparent evil in his life for a good purpose (Gen. 50:20). Moses waited until he was 80 years old before God used him to help deliver the Jews from Egypt. And even then, leading those faith-deficient people was a struggle (see Exodus).

Hebrews 11 lists people like Gideon, Samson, David, and Samuel, who saw great victories as they lived for the Lord. But in the middle of verse 35 the mood changes. Suddenly we are face-to-face with people who had to endure incredible suffering—people who died without seeing why God allowed them to undergo such tragedies. These individuals were tortured, jeered, flogged, stoned, cut in half, stabbed, mistreated, and forced to live as outcasts (vv.35-38). God had planned that only in the long-range view of eternity would their faithfulness during hardship be rewarded (vv. 39-40).

Pain forces us to look beyond our immediate circumstances. Suffering drives us to ask the big questions of "Why am I here?" and "What's the purpose of my life?" By pursuing those questions and finding the answers in the God of the Bible, we will find the stability we need to endure even the worst that life can inflict because we know that this present life is not all there is. When we understand that a sovereign God is standing over all of human history and weaving it all together in a beautiful tapestry that will ultimately glorify Him, then we can see things in better perspective.

> *"Faith is the substance of things hoped for, the evidence of things not seen."*
> —HEBREWS 11:1

In Romans 8:18 the apostle Paul wrote, "For I consider that the sufferings of this present time are not worthy to be compared with the glory which shall be revealed in us." Paul was not making light of our troubles, but he was telling believers to see our present troubles in light of all eternity. Our problems may indeed be heavy, even crushing. But Paul said that when compared to the incredible glories that await those who love God, even the darkest and most burdensome circumstances of life will fade by comparison.

We need to take time to look at one more example, perhaps the most significant illustration we could consider. The day that Christ hung on the cross is now referred to as Good Friday. At the time, it was anything but a good day. It was a day of intense suffering, anguish, darkness, and gloom. It was a day when Jesus felt all alone. It was a day when God seemed absent and silent, when evil seemed to triumph, and when hopes were dashed. But then came Sunday. Jesus rose from the grave. That awesome event put Friday in a different light. The resurrection gave a whole new meaning to what happened on the cross. Instead of being a time of defeat, it became a day of triumph.

We too can look ahead. We can endure our dark "Fridays" and be able to look on them as "good" because we serve the God of Sunday.

So when troubles strike, and they will, remember this: God uses such situations to direct us to Him and to the long-range view of life. He calls for us to trust, to hope, to wait.

TO SHAPE US

Athletic coaches like to use the phrase "No pain, no gain." As a high school track star (Okay, maybe I wasn't that great, but I tried hard!), I heard coaches remind us again and again that the tough practice sessions would pay off when we began to compete. They were right. Oh, we didn't always win, but our hard work did produce obvious benefits.

I learned a lot about myself during those years. And now I'm learning even more as I discipline myself to jog daily. Many days I would just as soon forget it. I don't want to have to feel the pain of stretching exercises. I would rather not push my body's "radiator system" to the extreme. I would just as soon not have to battle fatigue as I go up the hills.

So why do I do it? The gain *is* worth the pain. My blood pressure and pulse rate are kept low, my middle isn't expanding, and I feel more alert and healthy.

Exercise may have obvious benefits, but what about pain that we don't choose? What about illness, disease, accidents, and emotional agony? What kind of gain can come from those? Is the gain *really* worth the pain?

> *"Happy is he who has the God of Jacob for his help, whose hope is in the Lord his God, who made heaven and earth, the sea, and all that is in them."*
>
> —PSALM 146:5-6

Let's consider what a fellow-sufferer had to say in Romans 5:3-4. The apostle Paul wrote, "We also glory in tribulations, knowing that tribulation produces perseverance; and perseverance, character; and character, hope."

Paul introduced his statement about the benefits of suffering by saying "we also glory in tribulations." How could he say that we should rejoice or be happy that we are having to endure some painful tragedy? He certainly was not telling us to celebrate our troubles; rather, he was telling us to rejoice about what God can and will do for us and for His glory *through* our trials. Paul's statement encourages us to celebrate the end product, not the painful process itself. He did not mean we are to get some sort of morbid joy out of death, cancer, deformity, financial reversals, a broken relationship, or a tragic accident. All these things are awful—a dark reminder that we live in a world that has been corrupted by the curse of sin's effects.

The apostle James also wrote about how we should rejoice in the end result of our troubles. He said, "My brethren, count it all joy when you fall into various trials, knowing that the testing of your faith produces patience. But let patience have its perfect work, that you may be perfect and complete, lacking nothing" (1:2-4).

As we combine the truths of these two passages, we can see how the good and praiseworthy products of suffering are patient perseverance, maturity of character, and hope. God can use the hardships of life to shape us to be more mature in the faith, more godly, more Christlike.

When we trust Christ as our Savior, the Lord does not suddenly zap us so that we become perfect people. What He does is remove sin's penalty and set us on the road that leads to heaven. Life then becomes a time of character development as we learn more about God and how we are to please Him. Suffering has a way of dramatically forcing us to deal with the deeper issues of life. By doing so, we grow stronger and gain maturity.

My grandfather, Dr. M. R. De Haan, spoke about the shaping process of our lives in his book *Broken Things.* He wrote:

The greatest sermons I have ever heard were not preached from pulpits but from sickbeds. The greatest, deepest truths of God's Word have often been revealed not by those who preached as a result of their seminary preparation and education, but by those humble souls who have gone through the seminary of affliction and have learned experientially the deep things of the ways of God.

The most cheerful people I have met, with few exceptions, have been those who had the least sunshine and the most pain and suffering in their lives. The most grateful people I have met were not those who traveled a pathway of roses all their lives through, but those who were confined, because of circumstances, to their homes, often to their beds, and had learned to depend upon God as only such Christians know how to do. The gripers are usually, I have observed, those who enjoy excellent health. The complainers are those who have the least to complain about, and those dear saints of God who have refreshed my heart again and again as they preached from sickbed-pulpits have been the men and women who have been the most cheerful and the most grateful for the blessings of almighty God (pp. 43-44).

How have you responded to the difficulties of life? Have you become bitter or better? Have you grown in your faith or turned away from God? Have you become more Christlike in your character? Have you let your troubles shape you and conform you to the image of God's Son?

How Do All Things Work Together For Good?

Perhaps the most quoted part of the Bible during a time of pain and suffering is Romans 8:28. It reads, "We know that all things work together for good to those who love God, to those who are the called according to His purpose." This verse has often been misunderstood and perhaps misused, but its truth can bring a great deal of comfort.

The context of Romans 8 emphasizes what God is doing for us. The indwelling Holy Spirit gives us spiritual life (v.9), reassures us that we are children of God (v.16), and helps us with our prayers during our times of weakness (vv.26-27). Romans 8 also puts our sufferings in the bigger picture of what God is doing—that God is working out His plan of redemption (vv.18-26). Verses 28 through 39 reassure us of God's love for us, that no one or no thing could ever keep God from accomplishing what He wants to do, and that nothing could ever separate us from His love.

> *"Let patience have its perfect work, that you may be perfect and complete, lacking nothing."*
> —JAMES 1:4

Properly viewed in the context of Romans 8, then, verse 28 powerfully reassures us that God is working on behalf of all who have trusted His Son as Savior. The verse does not promise that we will understand all the events of life or that after a time of testing we will be blessed with good things in this life. But it does reassure us that God is working out His good plan through our lives. He is shaping us and our circumstances to bring glory to Himself.

Author Ron Lee Davis writes in his book *Becoming a Whole Person in a Broken World*, "The good news is not that God will make our circumstances come out the way we like, but that God can weave even our disappointments and disasters into His eternal plan. The evil that happens to us can be transformed into God's good. Romans 8:28 is God's guarantee that if we love God, our lives can be used to achieve His purposes and further His kingdom" (p. 122).

"But," you may ask, "how can God be in control when life seems so out of control? How can He be working things together for His glory and our ultimate good?" In his book *Why Us?* Warren Wiersbe states that God "proves His sovereignty, not by intervening constantly and preventing these events, but by ruling and overruling them so that even tragedies end up accomplishing His ultimate purposes" (p. 136).

As the sovereign Lord of the universe, God is using all of life to develop our maturity and Christlikeness, and to further His eternal plan. In order to accomplish those purposes, however, God wants to use us to help others, and He wants other people to help us. That's what the next section is all about.

TO UNITE US

Pain and suffering seem to have a special ability to show us how much we need each other. Our struggles remind us how fragile we really are. Even the weakness of others can bolster us when our own strength is sapped.

This truth becomes very real to me each time I meet with a small group of church friends for prayer and fellowship. During those regular times together, we have shared one another's burdens for a sick child, the loss of a job, workplace tensions, a rebellious child, a miscarriage, hostility among family members, depression, everyday stresses, an unsaved family member, tough decisions, neighborhood crime, battles with sin, and much more. Many times at the end of those meetings I have praised the Lord for the encouragement we have given to one another. We have been drawn closer and we have been strengthened as we have faced the struggles of life together.

These kinds of personal experiences in light of Scripture remind me of two key truths:

1. Suffering helps us to see our need of other believers.
2. Suffering helps us to meet the needs of others as we allow Christ to live through us.

Let's take a look two ways God uses pain and

suffering for the purpose of uniting us with other believers in Christ.

1. Suffering Helps Us To See Our Need Of Other Believers.

In describing the unity of all believers in Christ, the apostle Paul used the analogy of a human body (1 Cor. 12). He said that we need one another to function properly. Paul described the situation this way: "And if one member suffers, all the members suffer with it; or if one member is honored, all the members rejoice with it. Now you are the body of Christ, and members individually" (vv.26-27).

In his letter to the Ephesians, Paul spoke of Christ, "from whom the whole body, joined and knit together by what every joint supplies, according to the effective working by which every part does its share, causes growth of the body for the edifying of itself in love" (Eph. 4:16).

When we begin to recognize what other believers have to offer us, then we will realize how much can be gained by reaching out for their help when we are going through a time of struggle. When troubles seem to knock out our strength, we can lean on other believers to help us find new strength in the Lord's power.

2. Suffering Helps Us To Meet The Needs Of Others As We Allow Christ To Live Through Us.

In 2 Corinthians 1, the apostle Paul wrote, "Blessed be the God and Father of our Lord Jesus Christ, the Father of mercies and God of all comfort, who comforts us in all our tribulation, that we may be able to comfort those who are in any trouble, with the comfort with which we ourselves are comforted by God" (vv.3-4).

As we saw in the previous section, we need one another because we have something valuable to offer. We have acquired spiritual insights and wisdom as we have undergone trials of all sorts. We know the value of the personal presence of a loving person. When we experience the comfort of God during a troubling situation, we then have an ability to identify with those people who undergo similar situations.

While preparing to write this booklet, I read about the experiences of people who have suffered greatly, and I spoke with others who were familiar with pain. I searched to find out who helped them most in their time of trouble. The answer again and again has been this: another person who had undergone a similar experience. That person can empathize more fully, and his or her comments reflect understanding that comes by experience. To someone who is burdened down, it often sounds shallow and patronizing to hear another say, "I understand what you are going through," unless that person has gone through a similar situation.

> "In short, there is no magic cure for a person in pain. Mainly, such a person needs love, for love instinctively detects what is needed."
>
> —PHILIP YANCEY

Even though the best comforters are those who have undergone similar situations and have grown spiritually stronger through them, that does not mean that the rest of us are off the hook. All of us have a responsibility to do all we can to empathize, to try to understand, to try to comfort. Galatians 6:2 tells us, "Bear one another's burdens, and so fulfill the law of Christ." And Romans 12:15 states, "Rejoice with those who rejoice, and weep with those who weep."

Dr. Paul Brand, an expert on the disease of leprosy, wrote,

> When suffering strikes, those of us standing close by are flattened by the shock. We fight back the lumps in our throats, march resolutely to the hospital for visits, mumble a few cheerful words, perhaps look up articles on what to say to the grieving.
>
> But when I ask patients and their families, "Who helped you in your suffering?" I hear a strange, imprecise answer. The person described rarely has smooth answers and a winsome, effervescent personality. It is someone quiet, understanding, who listens more than talks, who does not judge or even offer much advice. "A sense of presence." "Someone there when I needed him." A hand to hold, an understanding, bewildered hug. A shared lump in the throat (*Fearfully and Wonderfully Made*, pp. 203-4).

It's clear—God made us to be dependent on one another. We have much to offer those in pain, and others have much to offer us as we endure troubles. As we develop that unity, we will experience greater comfort when we recognize that God uses suffering to alert us to the problems of sin, He uses difficulty to direct us to Him, and He can even use problems to make us more like Christ.

How Can We Help?

Right now you may be overwhelmed by pain.
The thought of trying to help someone else
may seem impossible. At some point along the way,
though, as you receive God's comfort, you will be
ready to give comfort (2 Cor. 1). In fact, reaching
out to help others may be an important part of the
process of your own emotional healing.

Or maybe you have read this booklet with the
hope that you will be better able to help a hurting
friend or loved one. The suggestions in this section
are designed for you as well.

Helping others is risky. Our help may not
always be welcomed. We may sometimes say the
wrong things. But try to help we must. Jesus' para-
ble of the Good Samaritan (Lk. 10:25-37) reminds
us that we are responsible to help the hurting people we encounter. Here are some suggestions:

- Don't wait for someone else to act first.
- Be present with them if possible and touch
  their hand or give an appropriate hug.
- Focus on their needs and not on your own
  discomfort with not having answers.
- Allow them to express their feelings. Don't
  condemn their emotions.
- Learn about their problem.

- Don't pretend that you never struggle.
- Keep your words brief.
- Avoid saying, "You shouldn't feel that way," or, "You know what you should do."
- Assure them of your prayers.
- Pray! Ask God to help you and them.
- Help them dispel false guilt by assuring them that suffering and sin are not inseparable.
- Help them find forgiveness in Christ if they are suffering due to sin or if they become aware of some sin in their lives.
- Encourage them to recall God's faithfulness in times past.
- Focus on Christ's example and help.
- Remind them that God loves us and cares for us and that He is in control.
- Encourage them to reach out for the help they need (friends, family, pastor).
- Help them to realize that coping with troubles takes time.
- Remind them of God's shepherding love (Ps. 23).
- Remind them of God's control over the universe—the big and small events of life.
- Don't ignore their problem.
- Don't be artificial in trying to "cheer them up." Be genuine. Be the friend you were to them before trouble hit.
- Show them the love you'd like other people to show you if you were in their situation.
- Be a good listener.

Better Than Answers

We cry out for complete answers. God offers Himself instead. And that's enough. If we know that we can trust Him, we don't need full explanations. It's enough to know that our pain and suffering are not meaningless. It's enough to know that God still rules the universe and that He really does care about us as individuals.

The greatest evidence of God's concern for us can be found by looking at Jesus Christ. God loved our suffering world so much that He sent His Son to agonize and die for us, to free us from being sentenced to eternal sorrow (Jn. 3:16-18). Because of Jesus, we can avoid the worst of all pain, the pain of separation from God—forever. And because of Christ, we can endure even the worst of tragedies now because of the strength He puts within us and the hope He sets before us.

The first step in coping realistically with the problem of suffering is to recognize its roots in the universal problem of sin. Have you recognized how much Jesus suffered on the cross for you to free you from the penalty of sin? Put your trust in Him. Receive His free gift of forgiveness. Only in Him will you find a lasting solution to the problem of pain in your life and in the world.

TWO

How Much Does God Control?

Our answer to this question will tell us a lot about our ability to trust God. It will show how ready we are to answer the objection of skeptics that the kind of all-powerful, good God described in the Bible is a logical impossibility. Such people argue that the amount of pain and suffering in the world proves that if God is good He's not all-powerful, and that if He's all-powerful He isn't good.

While the argument sounds philosophical, it's as real as the pain and fear that touches each of our lives and families. Herb Vander Lugt, who was RBC senior research editor when God called him home to heaven in 2006, understood some of these questions. In addition to more than 50 years of pastoral experience, he and his wife Ginny raised a dearly loved daughter who was brain injured at birth. I pray that you will find his conclusions, as reflected in the following pages, both comforting and challenging.

MARTIN R. DE HAAN II

How Much Does God Control?

A man who grew up in North Africa as the son of missionary parents tells of the time he saw a pregnant woman killed when a team of horses pulling a buggy galloped through a crowd of people. The driver stopped, saw that the woman was dead, shrugged his shoulders, and said, "It was the will of Allah," and continued on his way.

A 39-year-old woman has lost her desire to live because her husband left her for a younger lover. She has been a devout believer and wonders why God is doing this to her.

The grandfather of a teenage girl killed by a drunk driver has stopped going to church and becomes angry when people try to comfort him. He says that a good and all-powerful God would not let such things happen.

Sometimes it is hard to reconcile belief in God's goodness and power with what we see. I remember the thoughts and feelings I had as a young man when I visited a hospital's pediatric ward. As a surgical technician during World War II, I had seen severely wounded men. But the sight of deformed and dying children was almost too much for me. I couldn't think of any reason for what I saw. They had done nothing to bring these conditions on themselves. They could not learn anything through their pain. I found myself wondering about God, even doubting some of the beliefs I had cherished for most of my lifetime.

People who experience or observe debilitating disease or heartbreaking circumstances have a number of options. They can deny the existence of a personal God and struggle with unexplainable issues of origin and meaning. They can accept the existence of a God who is a mixture of good and evil. Or they can conclude that God is good, but that some things are beyond His control.

Another option is to become fatalistic. Many Christians have adopted a "whatever will be will be" attitude toward life. No matter what happens, it's God's will. Such a God may be feared, but how can He be loved? And if He cannot be loved, how can He be trusted? The implications are profound. Oswald Chambers made the astute observation that "the root of all sin is in the suspicion that God is not good."

The Bible gives us another choice, however. It presents God as both all-powerful and good. The God of the Bible is pleased with those who do good and slowly but surely becomes angry with those who stubbornly resist Him (Ps. 7:11; Nah. 1:1-7). He feels grief toward those who reject Him (Gen. 6:6; Ps. 95:10). He hurts when He finds it necessary to correct and punish (Isa. 63:9). He finds no pleasure in judging the wicked, and He longs for their change of heart (Ezek. 18:23,32; 33:11). He delights in kindness, justice, and righteousness (Jer. 9:24). And He loved the world so much that He appointed Jesus to take our punishment by dying like a sinner (Jn. 3:16).

People who have placed their trust in Jesus Christ and live in obedience to God's Word experience the reality of His love and love Him in return. They can go through overwhelming sorrows, distressing physical afflictions, and dire circumstances with amazing resiliency. The heartbroken father of a 20-year-old girl who died because the heater in the motel was not vented said to me, "I'm not angry with God. How can I doubt the goodness of the One who has shown so much love toward me and been so patient with me through all my years?" I talked with parents who had a teenage son and daughter both killed in separate accidents. They grieved deeply, but neither ever spoke bitterly or railed at anyone. They told me they anticipate heaven with a new eagerness and that they sense God's presence in their lives as never before.

The fact remains, however, that the world is full of grief, pain, sorrow, cruelty, and injustice. And while some believers are able to triumph over it, many are deeply shaken. They wonder where God is or why He lets them down. I have tried to help many such people and have suffered with them. I am therefore writing this booklet from my heart as well as my mind. I want to draw on the Bible and human experience to provide an understandable and practical answer to the question, "How Much Does God Control?" I will do so under the headings: (1) paradoxical truths, (2) conflicting kingdoms, (3) perplexing problems, and (4) practical implications.

Paradoxical Truths

The Bible doesn't tell us exactly how, when, or why evil came into God's world. What it does tell us, however, is everything we need to know to live hopefully and responsibly in this troubled world. It assures us that God is sovereign, that He is in control, and that He will carry out His loving plans and purposes for us. On the other hand, the Bible tells us that we are moral beings with the power of choice and that God holds us responsible to make good moral and spiritual decisions. How can both of these statements be true? It seems that they can't be unless we modify either God's sovereignty or human freedom. But the Bible doesn't allow us to take one path over the other.

GOD'S SOVEREIGNTY

God is all-powerful and so involved with what happens that not even a sparrow falls to the ground apart from His will (Mt. 10:29). He is in control of history. Paul declared that "He has made from one blood every nation of men to dwell on all the face of the earth, and has determined their preappointed times and the boundaries of their dwellings" (Acts 17:26). Paul also declared that the rulers of nations, bad as well as good, receive their authority from God (Dan. 4:17; Rom. 13:1). God decides to whom He will show mercy instead of wrath (Ex. 33:19; 34:5-7; Rom. 9:14-

24). He has chosen those who will be the redeemed in heaven (Jn. 6:37; Rom. 8:28-29; Eph. 1:4). He was involved when Pharaoh refused to listen to Moses and determined not to release the Israelites from slavery in his land (Ex. 5–14). He was even involved in the treachery of Judas Iscariot in that He provided the circumstances that made it possible for Judas to fulfill his preordained role (Acts 1:15-20).

God is active in history, even when He doesn't seem to be. This theme runs through the whole Bible. The Old Testament story of Joseph is a striking example. Joseph was indulged by his father, hated and abused by his brothers, falsely accused of sexually assaulting his employer's wife, and forgotten in prison. Yet through those dark years, God was quietly moving Joseph into a position to save the founding fathers of Israel from starvation. God gave Joseph the ability to interpret dreams, which put him in favor with the king of Egypt. And because of his God-given administrative ability, Joseph soon became the prime minister of Egypt. In this role, he was able to protect the nation of Egypt as well as his own family from famine.

More than 30 years after being the victim of his brothers' hatred, Joseph quieted their fear of retaliation by saying:

> Do not be afraid, for am I in the place of God? But as for you, you meant evil against me; but God meant it for good, in order to bring it about as it is this day, to save many people alive (Gen. 50:19-20).

God prospered the descendants of Jacob in Egypt.

They multiplied and became a nation of about 2.5 million people. He then allowed their circumstances to change when a new dynasty came into power. He brought Moses into the world, kept him alive, and through a succession of events trained and equipped him for the task of leading the Israelites. He supernaturally delivered them from their bondage from Egypt by sending 10 plagues and destroying Pharaoh's army. He then preserved them miraculously until they entered the Promised Land 40 years later.

God's part in what happens is not always detectable. His actions are often so interwoven with earthly and human factors that we do not know exactly what we can attribute directly to Him. We know that as a holy God who hates sin He never leads anyone to do evil. James declared as an absolute principle that "God cannot be tempted by evil, nor does He Himself tempt anyone" (1:13). Yet He works in and through human sin to accomplish His purposes.

He told the Israelites that if they disobeyed Him He would bring a nation against them and that the invaders would be unspeakably cruel (Dt. 28:49-52). The Bible writers repeatedly tell us that God sent the Assyrians and Babylonians against the Israelites. Moses also told the Israelites that God would bring them terrible plagues and sicknesses (vv.58-62).

A number of earthly and human factors were involved in the fulfillment of these threats. The leaders of the nations that attacked the Israelites freely chose to do it. The foreign invaders freely chose to be cruel and insensitive.

Perhaps some of the famines and plagues could be explained as natural events, but the Bible doesn't make these distinctions. God said they would take place in judgment, and He saw to it that they did. Maybe Satan and his kingdom of evil are so malignant that they quickly bring about pestilence and plagues as soon as God removes His restraining hand. Satan was eager to afflict Job and did so with vengeance as soon as God gave him permission. Job, not knowing the full story, attributed his suffering to God. Ultimately, of course, it had God's approval. He could have prevented it if He had chosen to do so.

Perhaps the relationship between Judas Iscariot and Jesus throws some light on the relationship between God and the evil ones He uses to carry out His plans. Knowing what Judas intended to do, Jesus hid this fact from His other disciples, told Judas to do quickly what he intended to do, and then went to the Garden where the betrayer could sell out for 30 pieces of silver.

The human heart needs no divine assistance to think about and carry out evil. All that is required is opportunity and a lack of restraint. An evil plan doesn't originate from God, but He may allow or even intervene to bring about circumstances favorable to the execution of the plan—as long as it accomplishes His purposes.

We can be certain that nothing can happen to us without passing through God's permissive will, and that He can bring about good through it (Rom. 8:28). With that assurance, we can live with trust and hope, no matter what our circumstances.

When doubts come, we can, like Job, talk to God about them with candor and honesty. As we grow to know Him better, we will see more and more clearly how great and good He is. We will also see how small and sinful we are. Finally, we will end all our complaining and say with Job, "I have heard of You by the hearing of the ear, but now my eye sees You. Therefore, I abhor myself, and repent in dust and ashes" (42:5-6).

God is sovereign. He is completely in control at all times. And those who know Him look forward to the day when they will join all the inhabitants of the universe to sing, "Blessing and honor and glory and power be to Him who sits on the throne, and to the Lamb, forever and ever!" (Rev. 5:13).

HUMAN FREEDOM

Under God's sovereign oversight, we are also free moral agents. We can and do choose between right and wrong, between good and evil. The Bible says that man was created in God's image and therefore possesses abilities and responsibilities not shared by any other earthly creatures.

- We have a unique level of understanding.
- We have a unique ability to make moral choices.
- We have a unique capacity to consciously place the interests of others ahead of our own; to love with the kind of love God has.

Our uniqueness can be seen clearly when we consider our ability to respond to our Lord's summary of the Law and Prophets: to love God above all and to love our neighbor as ourselves (Mt. 22:37-40).

As human beings we can, first of all, understand what these commands mean. We can evaluate their implications for our daily lives. We do not need much education or intelligence to do this.

Second, as human beings we can choose whether or not we will take these commands seriously. If we make the right choice and find that we cannot do so perfectly, we can choose to seek God's forgiveness and enablement.

Third, we can, with God's help, place the interests of others above our own. People sometimes go to great lengths and personal sacrifice to help those for whom they have no natural affection. Some have even given their lives for enemies. This is not true of the animal world, which has not been made in the likeness of God.

Since human beings are able to understand God's commands, we can choose whether or not to take them seriously. And since we have been given the ability to deliberately place the desires of others before our own, we are responsible when we do things that are ungodly, cruel, immoral, and selfish. Therefore, we have no right to blame God for our sins. Nor can we blame Him when someone wrongs us or perpetrates a terrible crime. Most human suffering is caused by people wronging other people. It is the result of wrong choices by people who could have done better.

Even though God is not surprised by our misuse of freedom, He enters emotionally into our failure. When He confronted Adam and Eve after they had sinned, He reflected disappointment as He called out to them, "Where are you?" (Gen. 3:9). Later He pled with Cain to resist his evil desire to kill Abel (4:6-7), but to no avail. A few chapters later, God observed that people had become so terribly wicked that He was "sorry that He had made man on the earth, and He was grieved in His heart" (6:6).

We ask, "God was sorry? Didn't He know what would happen?" But Moses felt no need to explain. A few thousand years later, about 1500 BC, God was repeatedly grieved and disappointed by the Israelites, a nation of people He had miraculously delivered out of slavery in Egypt. He had great plans for this nation. He told them He wanted to make them a "special treasure," "a kingdom of priests and a holy nation" (Ex. 19:5-6). He promised them that if they would obey Him they would be "blessed above all peoples," and He said He would "take away from [them] all sickness" (Dt. 7:12-16). Through the Israelites, God desired to make Himself known to the surrounding pagan nations. But they would not comply with the terms of obedience that would have made them "a light to the Gentiles" (Acts 13:47).

How did God feel when His people disobeyed Him and brought all kinds of trouble on themselves? He was angry (Ps. 95:8-11). He suffered with them and felt sorrow: "In all their affliction He was afflicted .... But they rebelled and grieved His Holy Spirit"

(Isa. 63:9-10). He felt like a loving husband does when his wife becomes unfaithful and refuses to change her ways until he has no choice but to divorce her: "How can I give you up, Ephraim? How can I hand you over, Israel? . . . . My heart churns within Me" (Hos. 11:8). He felt like a kind father does when his children are disrespectful and ungrateful: "A son honors his father . . . . If then I am the Father, where is My honor?" (Mal. 1:6).

The New Testament also portrayed God as disappointed, grieved, and frustrated. Jesus "came to His own, and His own did not receive Him" (Jn. 1:11). He repeatedly announced to the Israelites that He was the Messiah promised in the Old Testament. He performed miracles as evidence of the truthfulness of His claims, but He was hated, maligned, rejected, and finally crucified as a blasphemer. Matthew showed us how much this disappointed Jesus Christ, and how grieved He was as He contemplated the judgment that would fall on the generation that rejected Him:

O Jerusalem, Jerusalem . . . ! How often I wanted to gather your children together, as a hen gathers her chicks under her wings, but you were not willing! See! Your house is left to you desolate (Mt. 23:37-38).

Luke portrayed Jesus approaching the city near the close of His earthly ministry, weeping over it, and saying:

If you had known . . . the things that make for your peace! But now they are hidden from your eyes. For

*the days will come upon you when your enemies will
...surround you...and level you, and your children
within you, to the ground...because you did not know
the time of your visitation (Lk. 19:42-44).*

Remember, when you see and hear Jesus in the
Gospels, you are looking at and listening to God.
He said, "He who has seen Me has seen the Father"
(Jn. 14:9). Think of what this means! Are you heart-
sick and distressed by the wickedness, injustice,
pain, and sorrow around you? So is God! Are you
heartbroken because you are being wronged? Do
you wonder why God is allowing this grief? If so, be
assured that an evil person or evil people are doing
this to you. God isn't leading them to do these
wrongs. He hates to see you wronged. He feels
your grief. He holds the person or people wronging
you responsible for what they are doing. And He is
able to bring eternal good for you out of this bad
experience (Ps. 42). Therefore, quit blaming God.
Pray to Him. Trust Him. Take whatever appropriate
action is open to you. Then wait for God to prove
Himself faithful.

As we confront life with its pleasures and its
pains, its beauty and its ugliness, its goodness and its
evil, we hold to two truths: (1) our good God is
absolutely in control, and (2) we are free moral
agents who can choose to accept or reject God's
assistance in dealing with right and wrong. All too
often we make the wrong choices. When we do, we
grieve and disappoint God. But He is never surprised
or worried. He is firmly in charge. He can and He

does use even the sin of those who rebel against Him to chasten His people when they are disobedient, to punish the wicked, and to accomplish His purposes.

Sometimes God doesn't intervene as we might wish He would. The prophet Habakkuk was troubled by God's failure to punish the wicked in Israel. He called the Lord's attention to their wickedness. God told His servant that judgment was coming. The Babylonian armies would soon invade the land. This puzzled the prophet. Why help the Babylonians, a wicked and cruel people more godless and cruel than the Israelites? God then assured the prophet that He would also punish them in His own time. The prophet finally felt so confident about God's goodness and power that he closed his book with a hymn of praise and trust (Hab. 3:17-19).

The prophet Ezekiel, who was among the exiles after Babylon defeated the kingdom of Judah, was God's mouthpiece to tell the Lord's people that though they had "defiled" the land with their sin and "profaned" God's name wherever they went, they would one day repent, be cleansed, receive a new heart, and fulfill their destiny (Ezek. 36:16-38). He assured them that God is completely in charge.

When God came to earth in the person of Jesus Christ and presented Himself as Israel's promised Messiah, He was rejected and crucified. But God was not dismayed. He, of course, had known this would happen. He made Christ's crucifixion and resurrection the means of salvation and eternal glory for all who would believe. A little more than 7 weeks after our Lord's death and resurrection, the apostle Peter summed up this amazing truth in Acts 2:22-24.

Although people acted freely when they rejected and crucified the Son of God, they were not in charge of the universe. God was, and He used their rebellion to accomplish His goal.

The classic picture of God's sovereignty over man's rebellion is found in Psalm 2. It opens with a confederacy of nations in rebellion against God. They rage against Him and declare that they will break loose from His chains. But the Supreme Ruler does not feel threatened. He laughs in derision at the puny little kings. His laughter quickly turns to anger as He tells these rebels that He has already installed His Son as King. Then, warning these earthly rulers against continued rebellion, He urges them to serve Him with fear and surrender to His Son.

Human beings are free to oppose or to accept God. But God is completely in control. Nothing can happen unless He permits it. And in the end He will abolish all evil, right every wrong, and give those who trust Him an eternity of unmixed joy. That's comforting!

Conflicting Kingdoms

While the Bible clearly depicts God as sovereign, it also portrays Him in conflict with a hostile power. His enemy is Satan, whose power is so great that he is called the "ruler of this world" (Jn. 12:31; 14:30; 16:11) and the "god of this age" (2 Cor. 4:4). Paul used the word *exousia* three times to denote his authority over the realm of "darkness" and "the air" (Acts 26:18; Eph. 2:1-2; Col. 1:13). The "whole world lies under the sway of the wicked one" (1 Jn. 5:19).

Since Satan has authority over a vast realm, he heads a kingdom of evil that battles the kingdom of God. The evidence that these two kingdoms are in conflict is all around us—to some extent in nature, but far more pervasively in the moral and spiritual attitudes and actions of mankind.

The people who have chosen the kingdom of darkness reflect the spirit of their leader, the devil. Jesus said of him, "He was a murderer from the beginning . . . . When he speaks a lie, he speaks from his own resources, for he is a liar and the father of it" (Jn. 8:44).

Those who choose God as their King reflect the spirit of their Leader—the One who is the Author of life, the One in whom "we live and move and have our being" (Acts 17:28), and the One "who cannot lie" (Ti. 1:2). The fact that the kingdom of darkness wields great power accounts for a large share of the sin and suffering that mars our planet.

THE KINGDOM OF GOD

The Bible often speaks of the "kingdom of God." Sometimes it's depicted as an entity that always has and always will exist. The psalmist declared, "The Lord has established His throne in heaven, and His kingdom rules over all" (103:19) and "Your kingdom is an everlasting kingdom, and Your dominion endures throughout all generations" (145:13). Nothing in heaven, on earth, or in the underworld is outside the scope of God's rule. Even the devil can do only what God permits (Job 1:12; 2:6). Moreover, it is God who provides rain and fruitful season (Lev. 26:4-5; Dt. 28:12; Isa. 30:23; Acts 14:17). He is the ultimate source of all that is good, pleasant, just, and fair (Ps. 34). And while He normally exercises His control through natural processes, He intervenes with obvious miracles whenever He chooses. He sent the 10 plagues on Egypt, dried up the Red Sea, and fed 2.5 million Israelites with manna for 40 years. Whether by supernatural intervention or natural means, it makes little difference.

> *Whatever the Lord pleases He does, in heaven and in earth, in the seas and in all deep places. He causes the vapors to ascend from the ends of the earth; He makes lightning for the rain; He brings the wind out of His treasuries. He destroyed the firstborn of Egypt, both of man and beast. He sent signs and wonders into the*

midst of you, O Egypt, upon Pharaoh and all his ser-
vants (Ps. 135:6-9).

Isaiah declared that the king of Assyria was God's "rod," "staff," "ax," and "saw" to punish the citizens of the two tribes for their disobedience and rebellion (Isa. 10:5-15). The king did so with a free and self-centered choice, with no desire to fulfill God's will.

Jeremiah declared that Jehovah had "raised up the spirit of the kings of the Medes" to destroy Babylon (Jer. 51:11,28-37). Whether God did so directly or simply allowed their desire for power to take hold of them is not stated in the Bible. Therefore, all speculation is useless.

It's also useless to argue about the chronological order of God's foreknowledge and determined will. Theologians have debated this matter but haven't settled the issue. Since God sees everything—past, present, and future—with equal clarity, we finite, time-bound creatures are not capable of placing a chronological order to God's ways. Whether God exercises control through natural means or through His supernatural power is not always evident to us. But that doesn't matter. Either way, "His kingdom rules over all" (Ps. 103:19).

The phrase "kingdom of God" sometimes denotes a spiritual realm that exists now. We enter this "rule of God" when we believe on Jesus Christ. Paul declared that believers have been delivered "from the power of darkness and conveyed . . . into the kingdom of the Son of His love" (Col. 1:13). Jesus enunciated the principles of this kingdom in His Sermon on the Mount recorded in Matthew 5–7 and Luke 6:20-49. Paul said that the kingdom of God is "righteousness and peace and joy in the Holy Spirit" (Rom. 14:17). Those who enter this rule of God, therefore, are to be marked by their love, honesty, kindness, peaceableness, and readiness to forgive and go the extra mile for others.

The "kingdom of God" can also refer to a future physical realm. Someday (maybe soon) Jesus is going to return to earth to establish His kingdom of universal justice, righteousness, and peace. Old Testament prophets often spoke of this coming time. It will be a time of spiritual blessing (Isa. 32:1-2; Jer. 23:6; Ezek. 36:26-38) and a time during which perfect justice will be administrated (Isa. 2:1-4; 32:5; Mal. 3:18). Warfare will be abolished (Isa. 9:6-7; Hos. 2:18; Mic. 4:3). Social justice will prevail (Isa. 65:21-22; Amos 9:11,14). The climate will cause waste places to bloom (Isa. 35:1-2). Diseases and physical handicaps will be taken away (Isa. 35:5-6).

The fact that people who now voluntarily enter God's kingdom are to be marked by love, purity, kindness, and a forgiving spirit tells us what God is like. The fact that His coming kingdom will be free from injustice, war, natural disaster, and disease shows us the conditions that delight God. War, disease, injustice, natural disaster, and other evils are therefore present with us only because sin invaded the good world He created.

THE KINGDOM OF EVIL

As noted earlier, the Bible often refers to an evil

being called Satan, or the devil, who heads a kingdom of evil. Paul described his kingdom as well-organized when he wrote:

> *For we do not wrestle against flesh and blood, but against principalities, against powers, against the rulers of the darkness of this age, against spiritual hosts of wickedness in the heavenly places (Eph. 6:12).*

The Bible doesn't tell us when Satan became God's enemy. In fact, it doesn't describe his fall from sinlessness. It only alludes to it in Isaiah 14:12-15 and Ezekiel 28:12-19, passages that refer directly to the king of Babylon and the king of Tyre. When Satan rebelled, he apparently drew a great number of angels with him (Rev. 12:4). These fallen angels (called demons) are now his assistants.

Satan afflicted Job (Job 1–2). He moved David to become proud and to number the citizens of his nation (1 Chr. 21:1). An evil spirit, a member of Satan's army, became a "lying spirit" in the mouth of Ahab's prophets to persuade him to fight a battle in which he would be killed (1 Ki. 22:13-28). Powerful evil spirits empower and guide leaders of nations (Dan. 10:13). Evil spirits possessed people at the time of Christ and perhaps still do (Mt. 8:16-17,28-34). The devil and demons exercise real power through human agents who engage in idolatry and sorcery (1 Cor. 10:20). They empower false teachers (2 Cor. 11:13-14). They are able to work lying wonders (2 Th. 2:9; Rev. 18:23).

This kingdom of evil is pervasive and powerful. Satan and his agents are undoubtedly responsible for much of the evil in the world. They are malignant and hateful. They are undoubtedly involved in the wars, injustices, persecutions, plagues, and other forms of evil that mar our world. Yet they can do only what God permits. Therefore, the Bible writers sometimes ascribed to God the evils that came about through the agency of evil spirits. We see this when we compare 1 Chronicles 21:1 with 2 Samuel 24:1. We also find that Job saw his afflictions as coming from the Lord. But God never said, "Don't blame Me, the devil did it." Ultimately, God did permit it.

It's still important, however, to observe that much of the evil in our world comes from the devil and his agents. This reality enables us to maintain the doctrine that God is sinless and that He never instigates moral or spiritual evil. God's permission is not the same as His causation. Paul declared that God abandoned rebellious sinners to foolishness (Rom. 1:22), sensualism (vv.24-25), homosexual perversions (vv.26-27), a debased mind (vv.28-29), and total heartlessness (vv.30-32).

God didn't cause these sinners to go ever deeper and deeper into degradation. He permitted them. Is it not possible that as God observes humans going deeper into sin and rebellion that He gives the devil and his angels permission to bring about natural disasters, destructive crimes, and wars, persecutions, false religions, and plagues?

Perplexing Problems

C. S. Lewis has given good reasons for his contention that wars, crimes, and injustices—evils that come about through bad choices made by cruel and lawless people—account for at least 80 percent of mankind's suffering. Many believe he was too conservative in his estimate. Furthermore, the Bible shows us that sometimes wars, famines, and diseases are brought on by God as punishment for deliberate sin and unbelief. However, some tough questions remain to be answered.

- Why does God allow evil?
- Why does God allow disaster and disease?
- Why does God permit human history to continue generation after generation, even though most of mankind will die without faith in Christ and go to an eternal hell?

Why Does God Allow Evil?

Even if it is conceded that we are fallen creatures, we sometimes wonder why the Almighty permits some people to be so desperately wicked and heartless. Slavery, torture, murder, violence, and gross immorality testify to our awful wickedness. Why doesn't God stop people when they are about to do something extremely cruel or immoral? Undoubtedly He does sometimes. But not always. If He blocked all evil, He would take away the solemn fact that the nurturing of hateful or immoral thoughts is likely to produce actual murders and self-destructive acts. He would unmake human beings. He would remove our opportunity to trust Him in the best and worst of circumstances.

The human race is what it is today because the people who once "knew God" turned away from Him and began to worship idols and commit immoral deeds (Rom. 1:21-23). God then "gave them up to uncleanness" (v.24), "vile passions" (v.26), and a "debased mind" (v.28). But even while God abandoned them to their evil ways, He gave them a knowledge of "the righteous judgment of God." But they continued in their wickedness and encouraged others to join them (v.32).

God did not in any sense make people as self-centered as they are. He created our first parents good and healthy in heart (Eph. 4:24). But once sin entered the human family, it spread like industrial waste in a pure stream. The pollution became so pervasive that mankind would have lost every trace of goodness were it not for God's restraining presence.

Why Does God Allow Disaster And Disease?

While we can grow spiritually through suffering (Heb. 12:6), we sometimes encounter afflictions that seem cruel and useless. Who benefits when a grotesquely deformed baby is born? What good can come from severe retardation? What purpose can be served by an aged person going on month after month in an almost vegetative state? Why does the stroke victim who cannot speak or use his limbs have to lie in a nursing home year after year? And what about the victims of accidents or disasters?

We must admit that sometimes we can see no reason or purpose in some of the suffering we encounter. But that doesn't mean there is no divine reason or purpose. We just don't see it. Jesus said that a man was born blind, not because of sin on the part of anyone, but "that the works of God should be revealed in him" (Jn. 9:3). Then He went on to heal him supernaturally. Until that moment, no one knew why the man was born blind. But God did. Therefore, we must often rest in the assurance that God knows the answer to the question "Why?"

Then too, these disturbing realities are a call to repentance. They remind us that this life is only a tiny segment of the whole picture. Jesus pointed out that the 18 people who were killed when a tower fell on them were not singled out for this accident because they were worse than average sinners. But He went on to say, "Unless you repent you will all likewise perish" (Lk. 13:5). Whenever we encounter diseases, deformities, disasters, or accident victims, we are to remember that we are no better than they. This is therefore a call to repentance for all of us.

Something else that can help us when we come face-to-face with these disturbing facts of life is the realization that (1) God did not necessarily cause these circumstances and that (2) God suffers with the hurting. The world as we know it today is under the curse God pronounced at the dawn of human history (Gen. 3:17-19). Paul personified the non-human created world, animate and inanimate, as waiting eagerly for the day when Christ returns, because it will then be delivered from the frustration and pain it endures because of evil (Rom. 8:18-25).

Sometime in the past, either in connection with the fall of Satan or Adam, God introduced or permitted an element of disorder to enter the world. An elementary student of geology knows that the crust of the earth is a vast graveyard of species that came into being but did not survive very long. Scientists usually refer to the cause for this as randomness because it appears that way to us. (But not to God.) Maybe this element of disorder is the immediate cause of much of this world's distress—natural disasters, accidents, birth deformities, and debilitating diseases.

It's a fact that known genetic factors make it possible to predict that some families will have members with diabetes, heart disease, cancer, and other maladies. We may perhaps refer to a "naturalistic norm," meaning that God normally permits nature to have its way. He's running that kind of world. But as He allows this, He is also involved in every situation. And He doesn't enjoy seeing people endure grief and pain.

When Jesus was here as God incarnate, He showed us the heavenly Father's attitude toward diseases and handicaps. He treated them as enemies—healing the sick, giving sight to the blind, enabling the crippled to use their limbs. The apostle John told us that upon seeing the mourners weeping because of

Lazarus' death, Jesus "was deeply moved in spirit and troubled" (Jn. 11:33 NIV).

Many scholars point out that the Greek word translated "was troubled" often denotes anger. Alongside His sorrow (He was "deeply moved"), He felt a sense of indignation and anger. This feeling apparently swept over Him as He thought of all the pain and grief Satan and sin had brought into the world.

It helps us when we realize that much of the pain and sorrow of our sin-invaded world comes about through natural agencies or through God's enemies. But most of all, it's comforting to know that God is in control and that He suffers with us. Believing that He has good reasons for all that happens helps us, even though we cannot see those reasons.

Moreover, let's be careful to avoid overstating the harsh, unpleasant, and painful in life. Most people, including those who live in dire poverty or endure daily pain or cope with severe handicaps, enjoy life enough to want to continue living.

Yes, there is a lot of suffering. But we suffer one-by-one, and we receive grace when we look to God. Yes, we sometimes sorrow deeply. But after a time, the pain diminishes enough for us to go on with life.

Why Does God Permit Human History To Continue Generation After Generation Even Though Most Of Mankind Will Die Without Faith In Christ And Go To An Eternal Hell?

We are in no position to accuse God of being cruel because He lets human history continue. The apostle

Peter declared that it is a sign of God's patient love, because He is "not willing that any should perish but that all should come to repentance" (2 Pet. 3:9). God gives added time so that all of those He has chosen will be saved.

The glory of heaven is so marvelous we cannot comprehend it. How good of God to be so patient! And just as we cannot conceive of heaven's glory, we cannot comprehend the eternal state of those who die as rebels against God. We do best to simply affirm the biblical teaching that the Almighty will be perfectly just and fair. Some will receive little punishment (Lk. 12:47-48). Paul declared that God will take into consideration all factors like available knowledge and opportunity (Rom. 2:1-16).

We would like to believe in universal salvation—that all people will eventually embrace Jesus Christ and accept God's only way of salvation—but the Bible does not allow us to take this view. We may even like to believe in annihilation for the lost after they are judged and punished, but this idea doesn't have biblical support either.

Eternal existence, even in hell, is a tribute to human uniqueness among creatures. It magnifies the importance of our decisions. Some scholars have speculated that even in hell the inhabitants would choose continued consciousness to extinction of being. Maybe so. Maybe not. We join Abraham in asking the rhetorical question, "Shall not the Judge of all the earth do right?" (Gen. 18:25). And we can rest with the implied answer, "Yes, He will do right."

Practical Implications

L ife is difficult. At times it's hard to know what to believe. But God has not left us without light. Even in the darkness of natural disasters, devastating diseases, and heartbreaking injustices, God has placed within our hearts the knowledge of good and evil. Down deep, we sense our responsibility to choose to do right.

In this awareness God now invites us to respond to the light He has given us and to follow through in a life of love, obedience, and trust.

COMMIT YOURSELF TO THE LIGHT

The focal point of God's self-revelation came to our planet in the person of Jesus Christ. He shared our pain and felt our disappointments and grief. He lived sinlessly, but He died on the cross as if He were a sinner. He did this to take the punishment for our sins. Paul declared that "God made Him who had no sin to be sin for us, so that in Him we might become the righteousness of God" (2 Cor. 5:21 NIV). Then, on the third day after His crucifixion, Jesus left the tomb in a glorified human body.

All of this is well-confirmed history. The facts are well-attested. Therefore, acknowledging our sinfulness and believing what the Bible says about

Jesus Christ and salvation is not a blind leap into the dark. Rather, it's a step into the light. Jesus declared, "I tell you the truth, whoever hears My word and believes Him who sent Me has eternal life and will not be condemned; he has crossed over from death to life" (Jn. 5:24 NIV). The apostle Paul, whose conversion to faith in Christ is one of history's most significant events, wrote, "The word is near you ... the word of faith we are proclaiming: That if you confess with your mouth, 'Jesus is Lord,' and believe in your heart that God raised Him from the dead, you will be saved" (Rom. 10:8-9 NIV). Commitment to Christ is a walk into the light!

COMMIT YOURSELF TO LOVE

To be the kind of Christians who will experience God's goodness and the reality of His salvation, we must commit ourselves to a life marked by genuine love—love for God and love for others. Jesus summarized the demands of the Old Testament law:

> *You shall love the Lord your God with all your heart, with all your soul, and with all your mind. . . . You shall love your neighbor as yourself* (Mt. 22:37,39).

This means pleasing God more than pleasing ourselves. It means going out of our way to be kind, giving, and forgiving in all our earthly relationships. It means that by gifts of money and by voluntary service we will do what we can to reach people with the gospel, to feed the hungry, to provide shelter for the homeless, to rescue the fallen. We can do much to alleviate the suffering all around us. It is a life of submission to the challenge of Jesus:

> *If anyone would come after Me, he must deny himself and take up his cross daily and follow Me. For whoever wants to save his life will lose it, but whoever loses his life for Me will save it* (Lk. 9:23-24 NIV).

COMMIT YOURSELF TO OBEDIENCE

A commitment to obedience is almost automatic for a believer who is committed to love God and others. It means that we will look to the Scriptures for guidance and that we will strive to obey every command. We will pray because we are commanded to pray (1 Th. 5:17). We will respect and submit to governing authorities because we are commanded to do so (Rom. 13:1-7). We will take seriously our responsibilities as Christian citizens and stand up for truth and righteousness. We will submit to what the Bible says about marriage and divorce. We will respect plant and animal life, doing our best to carry out our responsibility to rule over and protect the earth as God's representatives (Gen. 1:26-28).

People who love and obey the Lord will be led to the joyous certainty: "If anyone loves Me, he will keep My word; and My Father will love him, and We will come to him and make Our home with him" (Jn. 14:23).

COMMIT YOURSELF TO TRUST

Christians are not exempt from pain and grief. Their loved ones die in car accidents just as others do.

They get cancer. When a natural disaster like an earthquake strikes, it hits believers as well as unbelievers. God does not make us His cosmic pets when we believe on Him. If He did, we could become complacent and proud. It would lead people to become Christians for the earthly benefits it brings. Job suffered and came to know God in a new way through his suffering.

In 2 Corinthians 11, Paul said that he suffered in the service of the Lord with repeated beatings, three shipwrecks, a stoning, hunger and cold, weariness and toil, and imprisonments. He then told of a "thorn in the flesh" and how he prayed three times for its removal, only to have God tell him the thorn would remain with him. But the Lord assured him, "My grace is sufficient for you, for My strength is made perfect in weakness" (2 Cor. 12:9). Paul was able to accept God's will joyfully:

> Therefore most gladly I will rather boast in my infirmities, that the power of Christ may rest upon me. Therefore I take pleasure in infirmities, in reproaches, in needs, in persecutions, in distresses, for Christ's sake. For when I am weak, then I am strong (2 Cor. 12:9-10).

The apostle Peter, writing to believers who were beginning to experience persecution, told them to expect and to accept bad treatment as Jesus did, without resentment or a desire to retaliate:

> When He was reviled, [He] did not revile in return; when He suffered, He did not threaten (1 Pet. 2:23).

Both Jesus and the apostle Paul reminded us that suffering is only for a little while, but glory is forever (Rom. 8:18; 2 Cor. 4:16-18; 1 Pet. 5:10). What did Jesus do when He faced the suffering associated with His trial and crucifixion? Peter said that He "committed Himself to Him who judges righteously" (1 Pet. 2:23).

What did Paul do in the midst of all his suffering? We saw that he trusted God and found it true that he was the strongest spiritually when he was the weakest physically. In a dungeon awaiting execution he could write with confidence:

For I am already being poured out as a drink offering, and the time of my departure is at hand. I have fought the good fight, I have finished the race, I have kept the faith. Finally, there is laid up for me the crown of righteousness, which the Lord, the righteous Judge, will give to me on that Day, and not to me only but also to all who have loved His appearing (2 Tim. 4:6-8).

Let's commit ourselves to trust God. If we do, we will find His grace adequate to give us victory over the worst that life can throw our way.

There are no easy answers. But we can commit ourselves to Christ and to a love-filled, obedient, and trusting way of life. And when we do, we can experience the truth of 1 John 5:4, "This is the victory that has overcome the world—our faith."

THREE

Does God Want Me Well?

Does God use sickness in the lives of His children to build character? Is this consistent with the actions of a loving God? Are we sick because we don't have the faith to be healed? Is God healing people today through the ministry of faith healers? When sickness or suffering attacks us or someone close to us, what should we think? What should we do?

These questions and many others like them are answered in the following pages written by Herb Vander Lugt. He shows what the Bible teaches about healing. And he uncovers four positive, unassailable certainties that every child of God can count on in times of sickness and suffering.

MARTIN R. DE HAAN II

The Problem Of Pain

The man responded angrily to my attempts to help. He was dying of lung cancer and was full of bitterness. He told me he didn't want to hear about a God who lets people suffer the way they do. He said, "I turned against the Bible and the Christian faith when my mother was dying of the same disease I have. She was a devout Christian, but in spite of her prayers she lived with terrible pain. I decided that either there isn't a God or that He isn't the kind of God you think He is."

My heart went out to him, but nothing I said made an impression on him. Finally I asked, "Did your mother turn away from God too?" He responded, "No, she kept talking about God's grace and about going to be with Jesus." Then he quickly added, "But I don't have the kind of faith she had."

Many people turn away from God because of the problem of pain. They find it hard to believe that a loving and all-powerful God would permit good people to suffer the way they do. On the other hand, thousands have testified that it was during a time of deep sorrow or intense anguish that they found God more real and precious than ever before.

Christians Agree
And Disagree

As Christians, we agree that God is loving, wise, and all-powerful. We agree that this good God gave His moral creatures freedom to choose between good and evil, and that their wrong choice brought His curse upon the earth. We also agree that this infinitely wise and good God is working out a program for our ultimate good and His glory.

However, even among us who believe the Bible, there are a few areas of disagreement. We give different answers to two very important questions, one having to do with the purpose of pain and the other with the matter of supernatural healing.

Does God Use Sickness To Make Good People Better?

Ken Blue, an evangelical Christian with an effective ministry in San Diego, says no. He writes:

> What we would call abuse in a human family, some have labeled a blessing in the family of God. Francis McNutt explains, "What human father or mother would choose cancer for their daughter to tame her pride?". . . One of the greatest hindrances to a vital healing ministry in the church today is the

notion that sickness is essentially good for us, that it is sent to purify the soul and build character . . . (*Authority to Heal*, InterVarsity Press, pp. 21-22).

On the other hand, Dr. M. R. De Haan, physician, minister, and founder of Radio Bible Class (now RBC Ministries), said that God *does* use sickness in the lives of His children to make them better. He wrote:

> The greatest sermons I have ever heard were not preached from pulpits, but from sickbeds. The greatest, deepest truths of God's Word have often been revealed . . . by humble souls who have gone through the seminary of affliction and have learned experientially the deep things of the ways of God.
>
> Are you afflicted and suffering, precious child of God? Then remember—your Father still knows best. . . . Grapes must be crushed before wine can be made. Unless the violin is stretched until it cries out in pain, there is no music in it. Wheat must be broken to make bread. We may not know what God is doing now, but someday we shall understand and be like Him (*Broken Things*, Discovery House Publishers, 1988, pp.44,91).

Is God Working Obvious Miracles Of Healing Today?

Dr. William Noland, after a period of diligent research, declared that he found no evidence that

God is working miraculous healings or that He has given any person the gift to do so. He writes:

> Two years ago I began looking for a healing miracle. When I started my search, I hoped to find some evidence that someone, somewhere, had supernatural powers that he or she would employ to cure those patients we doctors, with all our knowledge and training, must still label as "incurable." As I have said before, I have been unable to find any such miracle worker (*Healing: A Doctor in Search of a Miracle*, Fawcett, 1967, p. 272).

Dr. J. Sidlow Baxter, a well-known Bible teacher, says yes. He writes:

> The fact that many wonderful miracle healings are occurring today in great public healing rallies, who can deny? Only those deny who have not been and seen. With my own eyes almost jumping out of their sockets, I have seen the dumb from birth given speech, the stone-deaf given new hearing, the long blind suddenly given new vision, terminal cancer instantaneously cured (and later medically attested), crippled arthritics released and straightened on the spot, wheelchair victims of multiple sclerosis wheel their own chairs away, not to mention other such wonderful healings (*Divine Healing of the Body*, Zondervan, 1979, p. 270).

We can answer both of these questions with a solid yes. God does use suffering as a means of our spiritual advancement. Moreover, He does heal miraculously—but not always. And when He doesn't, we need not blame ourselves or give in to despair.

Biblical Certainties For Suffering Saints

She was a nurse and was quite sure she knew what she had. Yet her face blanched when the doctor came into the hospital room and said, "Sue, I hate to tell you what you already suspect is true. You have multiple sclerosis." She was aware of what she would be enduring—gradual paralysis, speech problems, impaired vision, jerking muscle tremors, and probably times of intense pain. It was not a pleasant prospect.

After the doctor left, Sue and her husband cried, but not for long. They prayed, talked to one another, and expressed their faith. As a result, they both sensed the presence of the Holy Spirit. They received strength to go on. Now, some 20 years later, they are doing quite well. The disease has progressed, but far more slowly than expected.

The essential elements of this scenario are occurring all the time. No family escapes completely unscathed. Not many, even among the most godly, enjoy excellent health until old age and then slip quietly off into the next world. It just doesn't work out that way. That is why we need to know what the Bible teaches about sickness and healing.

The following study will uncover four positive, unassailable certainties that every child of God can count on in times of sickness and suffering:

1. God will make you well.
2. God hurts when you hurt.
3. God knows why you're suffering.
4. God is in control.

GOD WILL MAKE YOU WELL

If you are a sick or suffering Christian, you can stand on the certainty that God will make you well—perhaps on earth, but surely in heaven. That's His guarantee. As His children, we are destined to receive a new, glorified body and to live forever in heaven. The apostle Paul drew tremendous comfort from his expectation of resurrection and eternal glory. After reaffirming the fact of Christ's resurrection in 1 Corinthians 15, he proceeded to point out that we too will receive resurrection bodies like the one Christ has (vv.20-58). In a spirit of joy and optimism he wrote:

We do not lose heart. Even though our outward man is perishing, yet the inward man is being renewed day by day. For our light affliction, which is but for a moment, is working for us a far more exceeding and eternal weight of glory, while we do not look at the things which are seen, but at the things which are not seen. For the things which are seen are temporary, but the things which are not seen are eternal. For we know that if our earthly house, this tent, is destroyed, we have a build-

ing from God, a house not made with hands, eternal in the heavens (2 Cor. 4:16—5:1).

Maybe you don't react to these words with much enthusiasm. You want healing in the here and now. Your feelings are not unusual. Suffering is not pleasant. We instinctively want good health and freedom from pain. We want it now. But when we let ourselves think this way, we are looking at life from the vantage point of those who have no real hope of heaven, those who tell us to grab all the gusto we can because "we only go around once."

That's wrong! Believers in Christ should live above the merely human level. We are to face squarely the fact that this life is brief at best and that things down here are never perfect. We are called on to exercise our faith and to look beyond the immediate and earthly. We will live forever in a wonderful new world! When we really grasp this truth, we can share the victorious attitude expressed by Paul in 2 Corinthians 4. We will begin to anticipate joyously the unseen and eternal realities of heaven. Indeed, we will "rejoice in hope of the glory of God" (Rom. 5:2).

Joel A. Freeman gives us an example of a person who learned to do this. He writes:

> Brian understands this principle. He has learned it the hard way. His 18-year-old eyes communicate mischief as he tries to run over my toes with his souped-up electric wheelchair. (Remind me to wear my steel-toed boots next time I visit him.)

Four years ago Brian was riding his 10-speed bicycle when a drunken driver careened across the median strip and hit him broadside. Brian pitched head over heels for 30 yards. The next thing he remembered was the soft touch of a nurse's hand on his forehead—5 days later.

As a paraplegic, Brian has battled the icy grip of self-pity. He's grappled with the seductive whisper of suicide. But you know what? He has won a tremendous victory—he has accepted God's sovereignty in the whole matter.

Brian's physical condition has made marginal improvements. His attitude, however, has made a 180-degree turn, from cyclical bouts with rage and hopelessness to sparkling eyes filled with an eternal purpose for living. He has become a "wounded healer" comforting others wherein he has been comforted (*God Is Not Fair,* Here's Life Publishers, p. 110).

No, Brian is not completely well physically. But he has experienced God's presence. He knows he is a member of that great body of suffering saints who have gone before (Heb. 11:30–12:4). This encourages him and makes him eager for the day when he will be completely well and with them.

GOD HURTS WHEN YOU HURT

If you are a suffering believer, the second biblical certainty from which you can draw great strength is the knowledge that God is suffering with you. He is not the "unmoved Mover" of Greek philosophy. He is not an unfeeling Being oblivious to the pain of His creatures. Nor is He a capricious Allah who carries out His will with no feeling for those who suffer. On the contrary, He is our loving heavenly Father. He hurts when we hurt. The psalmist declared, "As a father pities his children, so the Lord pities those who fear Him. For He knows our frame; He remembers that we are dust" (Ps. 103:13-14).

In reviewing God's dealings with Israel, the prophet wrote, "In all their affliction He was afflicted...; in His love and in His pity He redeemed them" (Isa. 63:9). The Old Testament prophets repeatedly pictured God as delighting in blessing His children and as grieving when they must suffer.

> *"Grapes must be crushed before wine can be made. Wheat must be broken to make bread."*

The truth that God hurts when we hurt did not find full expression, however, until it was revealed in the person of Jesus Christ. He is Immanuel, "God with us" (Isa. 7:14). He, the second person of the eternal Trinity, became a member of our humanity. He suffered everything we can suffer. He was born in a stable, a member of a poor family. He grew up in a humble home in a small village. He worked as a laboring man until He was 30. He didn't have a home during His 3 years of ministry. He was resented by His half brothers. He was rejected by the Jewish people to whom He came. He was misunderstood and misrepresented. He was mocked. He was falsely accused. He was betrayed by a close companion. He was forsaken by His closest friends. He was scourged. He was forced to carry a heavy wooden beam on His lacerated back. He was nailed to a cross. And even as He hung on it, He endured the taunts of mockers.

Why did He do all this? Couldn't He have paid the price for our sins without going through all of this humiliation and abuse? As far as we know, the answer is yes. His death on the cross, not His pre-Calvary suffering, atoned for our sin. It seems that He underwent all this added pain and humiliation for two reasons: to reveal God's heart (2 Cor. 4:6), and to become our sympathetic high priest (Heb. 4:15-16). God had always hurt when His people hurt. But He did so in a real, tangible manner through the incarnation—through the event that began in Bethlehem.

Are you suffering? Are you grieving? Are you disappointed because you are going to die before you can realize your plans and hopes? Be assured that God cares. He hurts with you. He doesn't like what you are enduring any more than you do. He could intervene and heal you instantly. But if He were to do this for you and every other person who is suffering, no one would have a need for the kind of faith that builds Christian character. Therefore, He allows you to suffer. But all the while He, like you, is looking forward to the time when all human pain will be over.

J. I. Packer has stated this truth eloquently:

God's love to sinners involves His identifying Himself with their needs. Such an identification is involved in all love: it is indeed the test of whether love is genuine or not.... It is not for nothing that the Bible habitually speaks of God as the loving Father and Husband of His

God does heal miraculously— but not always.

people. It follows from the very nature of these relationships that God's happiness will not be complete till all His beloved ones are finally out of trouble .... He has in effect resolved that henceforth for all eternity His happiness shall be conditional upon ours. Thus God saves not only for His glory, but for His gladness (*Knowing God*, InterVarsity Press, 1973, p. 113).

Just as a good husband suffers when he sees his wife in pain and loving parents feel the distress of their children, so also the Lord hurts when you hurt. And He won't be completely happy until you hurt no more.

GOD KNOWS WHY YOU'RE SUFFERING

This is the third comforting certainty. We want answers when we hurt, so we cry out, "Why?" God's special servants may even do this when grief or pain comes their way.

I know a minister who recently learned he had cancer. He was displeased with God's ways. He told a friend, "I can't understand why God let this happen to me. I've served Him faithfully. I'm not nurturing a secret sin. I've taken care of my body: I eat healthful foods. I avoid sweets, coffee, and soda pop. I keep my weight under control. I don't think I deserve this."

His protests remind us of those raised by Job almost 4,000 years ago. He hurled out the word *why* a total of 16 times. He even listed 12 ways in which he had been a moral, honest, kind, and loving man (Job 31:1-14). But God never answered Job's *why?* questions. Nor did He answer this query as it came from the lips of my minister friend. However, God did something better. He gave them the assurance that He knew why. He did so by reminding them of the great wisdom and power He displayed in His creation of the world. Moreover, He brought both of them to the place where they acknowledged His ways to be perfect in wisdom and goodness.

Sometimes we *can* answer the question why. It is always good to search our hearts to see if we bear some blame for our pain. We may be sick because we have not obeyed common-sense rules of health. Maybe the accident that hurt us is the result of our carelessness. It is also possible that our illness is the result of God's chastening because of sin in our lives (1 Cor. 11:29-30; Heb. 12:6). The Bible teaches us that some Christians die an untimely death (humanly speaking) because of sin (Acts 5:1-11; 1 Cor. 11:30). If we know we have been living disobediently, we must repent. God may give us healing when we do. And when we see the death of a believing loved one who has fallen into sinful ways, we can take comfort in the assurance that God sometimes takes one of His children home rather than see him continue on his destructive course.

However, we often can't find specific answers to our *why*? questions. We can't always expect to know the reason why we are suffering. But even then, God does not leave us completely in the dark. In addition to assuring us that He knows why, He has shown us that even unexplained suffering has a valuable purpose.

In John 9, Jesus used an encounter with a blind man to teach His disciples this lesson. They asked Him, "Rabbi, who sinned, this man or his parents, that he was born blind?" (v.2). They obviously saw this affliction as punishment for somebody's sin—either that of his parents or himself while he was still in the womb. Jesus answered them, "Neither this man nor his parents sinned, but that the works of God should be revealed in him" (v.3). This man's affliction was not punishment for any special sin. But it had value. It was designed to make him the vehicle through which God's power could be put on display. After He had made this point, Jesus said, "I must work the works of Him who sent Me while it is day; the night is coming when no one can work" (v.4). Then He gave the man his sight.

The application to us is obvious. Instead of wasting our energy in useless speculation about the why question, let's view suffering—our own or that which we encounter in others—as an opportunity to demonstrate God's power and bring glory to Him. Maybe He will answer our prayers by healing us. Perhaps He will use the suffering of someone we love to make us more compassionate, more kind, more helpful. Or He may let us suffer but give us such supernatural grace that we will be a vibrant testimony to His glory. Actually, God has many good reasons for letting us suffer:

- Suffering silences Satan (Job 1–2).
- Suffering gives God an opportunity to be glorified (Jn. 11:4).
- Suffering makes us more like Christ (Heb. 2:10; Phil. 3:10).
- Suffering makes us appreciative (Rom. 8:28).
- Suffering teaches us to depend on God (Ex. 14:13-14; Isa. 40:28-31).
- Suffering enables us to exercise our faith (Job 23:10; Rom. 8:24-25).
- Suffering teaches us patience (Rom. 5:3; Jas. 1:2-4).
- Suffering makes us sympathetic (2 Cor. 1:3-6).
- Suffering makes and keeps us humble (2 Cor. 12:7-10).
- Suffering brings rewards (2 Tim. 2:12; 1 Pet. 4:12-13).

Many other reasons for suffering could be given. We may not know which one fits our situation, but God does. That's comforting.

GOD IS IN CONTROL

This is the fourth biblical certainty for suffering believers. The fact that God is in control doesn't mean that He is the direct cause of every injury or disease. They sometimes come through Satan and usually through the outworking of natural laws that God has built into the universe.

Satan was the one who robbed Job of his possessions, children, and health. The woman Jesus healed from a crippling illness was "a daughter of Abraham, whom Satan has bound . . . for eighteen years" (Lk. 13:16). Satan was also involved in the "destruction of the flesh" in a disciplined church member (1 Cor. 5:5). And Paul's "thorn in the flesh" was a "messenger of Satan to buffet" him (2 Cor. 12:7).

Most suffering, however, is the result of natural processes. Habitual drunkenness leads to hallucinations, slurred speech, and physical collapse (Prov. 23:29-35). The young man entering the house of a prostitute is like an ox going into the slaughterhouse (Prov. 7:22). Timothy's stomach problems were probably related to the water he drank (1 Tim. 5:23). Many illnesses are eliminated through inoculations, diet, and good health habits. It's obvious that we cannot make God the primary agent in a large percentage of the suffering that plagues mankind.

The fact that Satan and natural factors are the direct agents in much human suffering, however, should not be taken as evidence that God is not involved. These evils would not have occurred if He hadn't permitted them. God gave the devil permission to afflict Job, but He set the limits (Job 1–2). Even when accidents or illness can be traced to human carelessness or natural causes, they occur because God allows them. Jesus assured us that nothing can happen to us unless it passes God's permissive will. He said that even a seemingly insignificant event like the death of a sparrow does not occur "apart from your Father's will" (Mt. 10:29). Paul expressed God's control of everything by declaring that we who believe are "predestined according to the purpose of Him who works all things according to the counsel of His will" (Eph. 1:11).

The truth that God hurts when we hurt did not find full expression until it was revealed in the person of Jesus Christ.

God has everything under His control. He may allow the devil to test you by making you sick. He may permit you to suffer great pain through an accident caused by carelessness or through a vicious attack by an evil person. These unpleasant events try us and may even tempt us to sin, but we can rest in the following assurance:

> *No temptation [test] has overtaken you except such as is common to man; but God is faithful, who will not allow you to be tempted beyond what you are able, but with the temptation will also make the way of escape, that you may be able to bear it (1 Cor. 10:13).*

No matter what your trial, no matter how great your pain or grief, remember that it passed the permissive will of your heavenly Father before it reached you. He loves you. He may heal you miraculously. If not, He will be with you in all your pain and someday take you to heaven. No matter what He does, He has your ultimate welfare in view. The perfectly wise and good God you serve has everything under control.

Sick And Suffering People In The Bible

The Bible gives us many accounts of severe illness, intense suffering, deep sorrow, and untimely death. These things are either attributed to God or to Satan. And on some occasions the source is not given. Sometimes healing came through a miracle. At other times, it came through a natural cure. And on some occasions, temporal healing didn't come at all—the person died. Sometimes the reason is stated. At other times it is implied. And on some occasions it is not indicated in any way.

JOB (Job 1–42)

- Identity—a godly and wealthy man who lived some 4,000 years ago (1:1-5).
- Affliction—loss of property, death of children, painful skin disease (1:13-19; 2:1-10).
- Source Of Affliction—Satan with God's permission (1:12; 2:6).
- Reason For Affliction—testing and refining (1:6-12; 2:1-10; 23:10).
- Result Of Affliction—greater knowledge of God and understanding of self (42:1-6).
- Lesson—God and Satan may both be involved in the sending of our afflictions (Job 1:12; 2:6).

MIRIAM (Ex. 15:20-21; Num. 12; 26:59)

- Identity—sister of Moses and Aaron.
- Affliction—leprosy.
- Source—God.
- Reason—chastening for rebellion.
- Result—repentance, healing, restoration.
- Lesson—God sometimes uses suffering to chasten His disobedient children.

EZEKIEL'S WIFE (Ezek. 24:15-27)

- Identity—wife of a major prophet.
- Affliction—her illness and death.
- Source—God.
- Reason—to illustrate God's dealings with the nation of Israel.
- Result—God was glorified (implied).
- Lesson—God sometimes uses suffering and even death to accomplish His purposes.

MEPHIBOSHETH (2 Sam. 4:4; 9)

- Identity—son of Jonathan; grandson of Saul.
- Affliction—crippled through a fall.
- Source—not given.
- Reason—not given.
- Result—lifetime affliction with no cure provided.
- Lesson—God doesn't always tell us the reason for our suffering.

PAUL (2 Cor. 12:1-10)

- Identity—the great apostle to the Gentiles.

- Affliction—a thorn in the flesh (an unidentified physical malady).
- Source—a gift from God (implied) and a "messenger of Satan."
- Reason—to keep Paul from exalting himself because of his unique spiritual experiences.
- Result—the thorn remained with Paul in spite of his prayers for deliverance but became a blessing because it increased his dependence on the Lord.
- Lesson—God doesn't always bring temporal healing, even to His most devoted children.

Questions On Healing

I n the following pages we will attempt to answer some common questions about healing that are often raised concerning certain biblical passages.

What About Our Authority To Heal?

In an *Our Daily Bread* article, I said that though we don't have the authority to call people back from death, we can do practical things to help those who are sorrowing. Much to my surprise, several people wrote me, accusing me of not believing Matthew 10:7-8, "As you go, preach, saying, 'The kingdom of heaven is at hand.' Heal the sick, cleanse the lepers, raise the dead, cast out demons. Freely you have received, freely give."

Yes, the Lord gave His disciples authority to heal, perhaps even to raise the dead (although these words are not found in some of the early manuscript copies). But we err if we make these words our marching orders or view them as giving us authority to heal the sick and raise the dead. They were addressed to a small group of men who at that time, on the other side of Calvary, were preaching the "gospel of the kingdom" to Jews only. After referring to this passage, Dr. De Haan, in his inimitable way, wrote:

They were not to accept money for their services; they were not to take any provision, but to live on the kindness and charity and generosity of the people to whom they ministered . . . . No lolling around in luxury for those apostles; no expensive hotel suites; but theirs was to be a life of rigor and self-denial; a life of poverty as became the followers of Him who had "nowhere to lay His head," who was born in a stable, depended on the charity of His friends, rode on a borrowed colt, and died on a sinner's cross. If, then, this commission in verse 8, "heal the sick," is to be taken for us today, it also should involve all of these other instructions which the Lord gave in this connection. This verse is constantly quoted as a reason for the same miracles today, but surely consistency alone demands that the rest of the passage be made to apply as well.

What About Healing In The Atonement?

"You need not be sick. Christ died for our sicknesses as well as our sins. Through faith we must claim freedom from illness just as we claim freedom from the penalty of our sins. That's what Matthew 8:16-17 tells us." A godly man dying of cancer heard a radio preacher say this. He became troubled. He began to suffer from a feeling of guilt about his lack of faith just as much as from his illness. I assured him that he had not failed spiritually. He and his loved ones had prayed earnestly. Neither their prayers nor their faith were deficient. It apparently was not God's will to heal him. The man was then able to face his approaching death with faith and courage.

Let's examine Matthew 8:16-17 to see exactly what it says about the relationships between the atonement and healing. We read:

> *When evening had come, they brought to Him many who were demon-possessed. And He cast out the spirits with a word, and healed all who were sick, that it might be fulfilled which was spoken by Isaiah the prophet, saying: "He Himself took our infirmities and bore our sicknesses."*

The closing words are an accurate quotation from the Hebrew text of Isaiah 53:4. Jesus "took" our sicknesses by sympathetically and compassionately entering into the pains and sorrows of mankind. His miracles of healing were signs. They showed His compassion for us and pointed forward to His death by which He would pay the price for sin so ultimately all suffering can end. His miracles of healing were signs of the complete healing that will be enjoyed ultimately by all who place their trust in Him.

Nothing in this passage even remotely suggests that we can claim physical healing through the atonement. In the *Expositor's Bible Commentary*, D. A. Carson astutely observed: "The cross is the basis for all the benefits which accrue to believers; but this does not mean that all such benefits can be secured at the present time on demand" (Vol. 8, p. 267).

What About Anointing services?

In some church services, sick and suffering people are invited to come forward to be anointed with oil and prayed for. This practice is based on James 5:13-16. But the sick person in James calls for the elders to come to him. Perhaps he is too ill to go to them. The combination of the Greek word *asthenia* (sick) in verse 14 and *kamno* (sick) in verse 15 is seen by some Bible students as portraying someone who is flat in bed, probably hopelessly ill. This anointing does not occur in a public service or on invitation from the platform.

The elders are to pray for the sick person and anoint him with oil. This anointing with oil was ceremonial, not medicinal. Oil had no healing value for a person with a severe, life-threatening illness. Besides, James said that it is the "prayer of faith," not the oil, that saves the sick from physical death.

What is this prayer of faith? It certainly isn't a state of mind a person acquires through a lot of agonized crying or shouting. That goes against what Jesus said about praying (Mt. 6:7-15). The "prayer of faith" is Spirit-led praying that is sensitive to God's will and submissive to it.

James 5:13-16 was addressed to saints in the church age. But some Bible students believe that it was intended only for people who lived during the apostolic era. They point out that James was written at a very early date while the apostles who possessed the gifts of healings and discernment (1 Cor. 12:1-11) were still living. They also call our attention to the fact that the text seems to imply that healing could always be expected.

Many other Bible students, however, are not comfortable with this interpretation. They can't find solid reasons to limit this instruction to the apostolic era. They therefore say that we should honor requests for anointing and prayer from those who are ill. They also point out that confession of sin seems to be an important element in this anointing and prayer service.

Bible scholars do indeed differ as to the value of this practice in the church today. However, one thing is certain. No fair-minded person can make it the biblical basis for public anointing services.

What About The Gift Of Healing?

Some Christian leaders are convinced that they possess the "gifts of healings" referred to in 1 Corinthians 12. Moreover, many sane, honest, and respectable people support this claim. They testify that they experienced or witnessed real healings through the laying on of hands in a healing service. And they challenge those who don't believe them to produce a New Testament verse that states explicitly that gifts of healings stopped with the apostles.

Now, it is true that the New Testament writers nowhere explicitly declare that the gifts of healings ceased. However, Hebrews 2:1-4 makes it clear that the miraculous sign-gifts were not present in about AD 68 as they were at an earlier stage in the apostolic era. The writer of Hebrews declared that the message of salvation "was confirmed . . . both with signs and wonders, with various miracles, and gifts of the Holy Spirit, according to His own will" (Heb. 2:3-4). He used the past tense. In addition, he lumped together "signs and wonders" and "gifts of the Spirit." It appears that the supernatural sign-gifts were no longer present to the extent that they were at an earlier time.

Another matter of significance is the fact that in the Greek language, the supernatural sign-gifts are written as double plurals—"gifts of healings," "gifts of tongues," "workings of miracles." This may indicate that the supernatural gifts did not reside in an individual like the gift of an office—apostle, prophet, evangelist, and pastor-teacher (Eph. 4:11). They apparently came upon a person for one event and had to be given again or renewed by the Holy Spirit according to His will. Perhaps that's why Paul, who on one occasion healed a host of people (Acts 19:11-12), couldn't heal Epaphroditus (Phil. 2:25-30), Trophimus (2 Tim. 4:20), or Timothy (1 Tim. 5:23).

Since even the apostles didn't possess a resident gift of healing, we have good reason to deny that anyone has it today. Then too, the recorded instances of miraculous healings during subsequent eras of church history should not be seen as evidence that the signs and wonders and gifts of healings continued. A divine healing need not be a sign or wonder, even if it is quite clearly supernatural. Nor do present healings through prayer indicate that somebody exercised the "gifts of healings." God can heal in response to prayer whenever He chooses to do so.

What About The Astounding Contemporary Reports Of Healing?

Wherever you go, you can find people who tell of being miraculously cured through prayer, through a visit to a shrine, or through the work of a healer. The tendency among non-Christians (and even many Christians) has been to disregard or deny these reports. Lately, however, many secularists are taking them more seriously without thinking of these unexplainable phenomena as divine miracles. They are quick to point out that spontaneous remissions and apparent healings occur among Christians and non-Christians. They find refuge in the mystery of the relationship between mind and matter and the unexplainable power of suggestion. They don't even attempt to refute testimonials of amazing healings by people who received treatment from quacks whose methods have no scientific validity.

Our approach as Christians is different. We believe in God and His power to heal. Many of us have had firsthand experiences of amazing healings in response to prayer. Therefore, we do not question the fact that God can and does heal. However, we should recognize that not all humanly unexplainable incidents are miracles of God. They occur even among Satan worshipers! Therefore, we test a religious leader's credibility by what he teaches, not by an analysis of the miracles ascribed to him or her.

What About Paul's "Thorn In The Flesh"?

In 2 Corinthians 12:1-10, Paul spoke of his "thorn in the flesh." He said that it was "given" him to keep him from becoming conceited because of the amazing revelations he had received. He also declared it to be "a messenger from Satan to buffet me." The giver of the thorn was undoubtedly God; He, not the devil, would be concerned to keep Paul humble. But Satan could use the thorn to distress him.

We don't know what the "thorn" was. A number of guesses have been made. Some have mentioned bad eyes, epilepsy, malaria. Others, eager to maintain that obedient Christians are free from disease, have mentioned an indwelling demon or bitter enemies. These last suggestions, however, don't fit Paul's words, "Therefore most gladly I will rather boast in my infirmities, that the power of Christ may rest upon me" (v.9). An indwelling demon or persistent enemies are not "weaknesses." The "thorn" was without question some kind of physical affliction. And God gave it to Paul for his spiritual good. God didn't remove it even though Paul prayed earnestly for its removal. But He provided such wonderful grace and strength that Paul saw it as a blessing.

How Much Faith Do I Need?

Many people have the idea that if we fulfill God's conditions by having enough faith, we will always be healed. Therefore they boldly "name and claim" complete healing when they pray. They even tell a person that he or she is well while the symptoms of the illness are still present.

Dr. Paul Brand in the November 25, 1983, issue of *Christianity Today* told the sad story about a family that took this approach. When their 15-month-old son came down with flu-like symptoms, they followed the advice of their church leaders and depended solely on prayer for his recovery. Their son kept getting more sick over the next several weeks, gradually losing his senses of hearing and sight. He finally died—and he remained dead in spite of fervent prayer that God would restore his life. The autopsy showed that the cause of death was a form of meningitis that could have been treated easily.

Jesus' miracles of healing were signs of the complete healing that will be enjoyed ultimately by all who place their trust in Him.

Now, these people had tremendous faith. But the strength of our faith does not determine whether or not healing will come. Some of our Lord's miracles were not in any way related to the faith of those who benefited from them (Mt. 12:9-13; Mk. 1:23-28; Lk. 7:11-15; 13:10-13; 14:1-6; 22:50-51; Jn. 9:1-38). Besides, are we going to say that Paul was not healed of his "thorn in the flesh" because he didn't have enough faith? Was Timothy's lack of faith the reason he had stomach problems? (1 Tim. 5:23).

Does God Want
Me Well?

We are now ready to answer directly the question, "Does God Want Me Well?". Yes, God wants you well—just as He "desires all men to be saved and to come to the knowledge of the truth" (1 Tim. 2:4). But not everyone accepts His offer of salvation. God would like to see His children well, but many of them disobey good health rules. Some fall into sinful ways and need to be chastened (Heb. 12:6). All of us are spiritually benefited by some trials and pain. Both Paul and James exhorted believers to be glad when they are tested by suffering (Rom. 5:3-5; Jas. 1:2-4). Their teachings assure us that it is an indispensable element in our spiritual development. God would like us well, but it would not be good for us to go through life without pain.

It does not follow, however, that we should take a dim view of physical health or pleasure. Nor should we stoically resign ourselves to the idea that we should expect a lot of suffering. On the contrary, we should look at life optimistically. God's Word provides assurances and promotes a way of life that is conducive to physical and psychological wellness. It does so in at least nine ways:

1. It brings relief from the heavy burden of guilt (Ps. 32:1-2; Rom. 5:1).
2. It provides the power to release inner bitterness caused by an unforgiving spirit (Mt. 6:12,14-15; Eph. 4:32).
3. It promotes a positive view toward our body, assuring us that the Holy Spirit lives in it (1 Cor. 6:19), and that it is destined for resurrection (1 Cor. 15).
4. It teaches that sexual expression is both safe and satisfying within marriage (1 Cor. 7:1-5; Heb. 13:4).
5. It provides grace for single believers, enabling them to live a happy and fulfilled life (1 Cor. 7:7-8,32,39-40).
6. It is marked by hope—a buoyant confidence about the future (Rom. 8:31-39).
7. It assures us that we are members of a select community—the body of Christ in which each person fills a special role for the mutual benefit of all (Rom. 12:3-8; 1 Cor. 12:1-31).
8. It fosters a unique relationship with God so that we can ask Him for healing when we are sick (Mt. 7:7-11; Rom. 8:15; Jas. 5:14-15).
9. It enables us to rejoice even when we suffer pain (Acts 5:41; 2 Cor. 4:16-18).

God wants you well. He allows illness and pain only when He can use them for your good. And He is going to see to it that you will be well for all eternity. Believing this will promote your good health.

Sickness, Healing, And You

If you have placed your trust in Jesus Christ, you can face bad news calmly and hopefully. If you are not living obediently, you can turn away from your sin and back to God. You can ask the Lord for healing. You can pray with the absolute assurance that God will heal you, if doing so will bring glory to Himself and further your eternal welfare. And if He doesn't make you well, He will give you His wonderful grace and use the affliction for good.

If you have never placed your trust in Jesus Christ, do it today. Acknowledge your sinfulness and your inability to save yourself. Believe that Jesus died on the cross for sinners and that He rose again. Then put your trust in Him. Believe that He did it for you. He will forgive you, make you a member of His family, and give you eternal life. He will take care of you through all time and eternity.

FOUR

When Tragedy Strikes

Tsunamis, hurricanes, and earthquakes have natural explanations that make no sense. Mindless fires take sleeping families. Troubled people murder people they don't even know. Accidents no one sees coming leave us with questions that have no human answers.

What are we to think or do when faced with loss that seems to challenge the meaning of life and the goodness of God? What is our response to be when tragedy strikes—whether on a national scale or within our own circle of friends and family?

Tim Jackson, a licensed counselor and a member of the RBC biblical correspondence team, hears such questions almost daily. Out of his experience and his faith in the wisdom of the Bible, Tim offers help in the following pages to those of us who find ourselves wondering where we are going to discover the strength, reason, and faith to carry on.

MARTIN R. DE HAAN II

When Tragedy Strikes

"Are you near a TV?" was the question my wife blurted out when I picked up the phone. "No," I responded, somewhat surprised that I didn't get the usual upbeat greeting from her. I was working at my desk as I would be on any normal Tuesday morning. "Get to one!" she insisted. "Two planes have just hit the World Trade Center towers in New York. They think it might be terrorists!"

Moments later I was huddled around a small TV monitor in a cramped video editing suite with a few co-workers. We stared in stunned silence as the images of United Flight 175 and American Flight 11 slashing into the two towers were replayed again and again. As we tried to absorb the enormity of what was happening, the south tower collapsed in a cloud of smoke and rubble. A short time later the north tower collapsed into itself. One moment they were there. Then they were gone, taking with them an unknown number of lives. For the rest of that day and many more to follow, I was glued to every newscast to learn as much as I could of the fate of those caught in what certainly has become one of the most surreal events I have ever seen. The horrific images I witnessed are forever etched in my memory.

The world changed that day for all of us. And not

just for those in the US. Terrorists served notice on 9/11 that there is no place on earth that is truly safe. If the last remaining superpower in the world could be hit with such a devastating blow, we're all vulnerable. As noted bereavement specialist Joanne Jozefowski remarked, "Whether or not we suffered a personal or peripheral loss, we have all lost something very valuable. We have lost our illusion of safety" (*The Phoenix Phenomenon*, p. 229).

When tragedy strikes, safety evaporates. Security is undermined. Uncertainty abounds. Fear invades. Human frailty is exposed. Faced with our own mortality, our vulnerability becomes an impenetrable fog that engulfs the human heart. But tragedy is not exclusively the result of terrorism. It can strike unannounced from just about any direction.

Individual losses of all kinds can change the lives of those who are directly affected. But some events, by their unexpected and horrific nature, inflict trauma on whole communities.

Tragedy strikes the deepest when it hits where we least expect it, ripping apart our sense of security and shaking us with feelings of loss and vulnerability.

What are we to think and feel when our own lives are touched by events of cataclysmic proportions? Will we lose all hope in the face of trouble over which we have no control? Or will we experience, as others have, that there are ways to survive and even grow in the face of natural disasters, catastrophic accidents, and violence?

Natural disasters are sudden, destructive events resulting in widespread and catastrophic loss of life and property. Events like

- tornadoes ripping through towns in the US heartland
- mudslides entombing a whole village in Costa Rica
- torrential flooding in Cambodia
- typhoons in Malaysia
- wildfires in the Canadian Rockies
- hurricanes in the Caribbean
- volcanic eruptions in the Philippines

Catastrophic accidents are unexpected and unintended events resulting in injury, loss, and damage. They are often caused by negligence or mechanical failures.

- automobile accidents
- work-related accidents
- home fires
- drownings

Violent tragedies are the result of intentional violence that targets an individual or group, such as

- assaults
- arson
- kidnappings
- murders
- terrorist attacks
- wars

In spite of all our efforts to make the world a safer place for ourselves and our children, it is marked by violence, disasters, and catastrophes.

A flurry of questions assaults us in the wake of such devastation: What do we have left when so much has been lost? How do we handle such tragedy? How can we survive? How do we feel? How are we *supposed* to feel? Will we ever feel safe again? Will things ever be normal again? How can we help each other through tragic events?

Many of us question how we would handle facing our vulnerability in the middle of a disaster. That's part of the attraction to films like *Titanic*.

Titanic remains the largest-grossing movie of all time, partly because it's a tragic love story set during a well-known disaster at sea that had both international significance and individual impact. That's true of all tragic events. We see them as huge events, bigger than life. But cataclysmic earth-shaking events are made up of many smaller, but no less significant, stories of real people discovering in the midst of uncertainty what matters most for those who remain.

Tragedy has a way of bringing out the worst and the best in us. The same events that bring looters into a devastated neighborhood become the occasion for others to reach out to help one another as they never have before. How we respond tells a lot about ourselves.

Some Common Characteristics Of Tragic Events

When we think of a tragedy, we don't think of someone who has lived a full life and dies in his mid-nineties with family and friends surrounding his deathbed. That's a painful loss to be sure, but we wouldn't describe it as tragic. It was expected. The outcome was predictable.

But the loss of life or property resulting from a horrific accident, an act of violence, or a natural disaster is what we usually think of as a tragedy. It was sudden and unexpected. Life was going along so well, normal by the standards of most, and then it was abruptly interrupted and forever changed without warning.

Like a bomb blast in a busy shopping mall or an earthquake that rumbles wildly, the devastation from a disastrous event spreads out for miles in every direction.

Joanne Jozefowski has identified some common characteristics of catastrophic events that are more likely to precipitate traumatic grief reactions (*The Phoenix Phenomenon*, pp. 230-31). As you review this list, think back over how many of these characteristics were present in events that you've directly or indirectly experienced.

They Are Unexpected.

They strike out of the blue, unleashing their fury without warning. We feel stunned and shocked, blindsided by a sucker-punch that leaves us dazed and disoriented. We feel overwhelmed and woefully unprepared.

They Are Uncontrollable.

The event not only takes us by surprise but it is also beyond our ability to prevent, change, or manage. We feel powerless to stop it once it starts and vulnerable because we know we couldn't have prevented it from happening.

They Are Unimaginable.

The devastating fallout from a tragic event is beyond our comprehension. We simply don't have a normal category for processing what we've experienced. We see it with our eyes, but we just can't believe it's really happening. It's this surreal quality of a tragedy that leaves us stunned by what we previously would have called "unthinkable."

Many people have described watching the events of 9/11 unfold on live TV as a surreal experience. The images seemed more like those from an action film than the real-life horrors of crashing planes and collapsing buildings. Thousands of people just like us got up to go to work that morning and never came home.

They Are Unprecedented.

Nothing like this has ever happened to us personally before. We often don't know what to do or how to respond because we've never faced anything quite like this. Without something to compare it to, we often feel lost, struggling for direction.

They Leave Us Uncertain And Vulnerable.

In the aftermath of a tragedy, life's fragility is glaringly apparent. No one fully understands the extensive and long-term impact a tragedy will have on us, our family, our livelihood, or our future. We feel torn between hope and fear, despair and disbelief. We don't want to give up hoping, and yet we're afraid to allow ourselves to dream or long for anything or anyone ever again.

One of the long-term effects of surviving a tragic event is the lingering feeling of our own vulnerability.

For the first 18 days of October 2002, nothing was certain as a pair of snipers terrorized the area surrounding Washington, DC. Their deadly shooting spree left 10 people dead, 3 critically wounded, and millions traumatized. The randomness of the victims (without regard for age, race, or sex), the ordinariness of the locations (malls, gas stations, parking lots, schools), and the devastating lethal outcome had everyone looking over their shoulder, not knowing who would be next.

I had a sense of what those in the community were feeling when I heard that one of the female victims had been gunned down outside of the exact store where my sister-in-law had been shopping just a few hours earlier.

In a world of pronounced danger and uncertainty, one thing is certain—*we're all at risk.* All the gun legislation, homeland security, and hi-tech surveillance equipment cannot guarantee absolute security against terrorist attacks. Effective geological research cannot prevent a devastating earthquake. Doppler radar and satellite imaging cannot hold back surging floodwaters, still a hurricane, or stop a deadly tornado. The issue isn't our ability to research and predict potential disasters; it's our inability to prevent and protect ourselves and loved ones from them.

How Do We Experience Our Vulnerability When Tragedy Strikes?

I didn't lose anyone in my family on 9/11, yet I felt stunned and vulnerable. But Lisa Beamer did lose someone. Her husband Todd was one of the passengers on the ill-fated United Flight 93. In her book *Let's Roll!* Lisa describes her initial feelings after she heard the news over the TV that Todd's plane had gone down in a Pennsylvania field.

> I made my way to my bedroom and sat down on the edge of the bed, staring out the window in a near-catatonic state. I didn't move; I didn't speak. It was as though time had come to an abrupt halt, and I no longer existed. In a desperate, futile attempt to make sense of it all, my heart and mind had temporarily shut down. I was numb. I could see and hear, yet I simply continued to stare straight ahead (pp. 10-11).

What Lisa experienced is normal. For someone who has been blindsided with the fateful news of a tragic loss or who has survived going through a disaster, confusion and disorientation are normal.

Some of the most common feelings that assault us in the aftermath of a tragedy are the following:

Shock

The initial high-voltage jolt of a catastrophe sends our whole system into a natural and necessary self-protection mode. Shock is a form of emotional numbness that sets in immediately after we witness, survive, or receive the news of a tragic event. It's the emotional circuit breaker that trips to protect us from a massive overload that could result in total shutdown and the inability to function.

Shock is experienced as going through the motions but not feeling fully present in the moment. Some people describe it as an out-of-body kind of experience, observing themselves without being able to respond. Others describe it as being in slow motion. They hear and see others around them, feel the urgency of the moment, but everything has drastically slowed down. Sounds are muted and may seem distant. Every movement feels agonizingly slow and labored.

Shock is the body's first line of defense against the overwhelming chaos of a tragedy. It's a short-term emotional disconnect, allowing us time to slowly absorb what has happened. But it can't prevent the hurt forever. The pain returns.

Pain

In spite of all our best efforts to prepare for it, nothing can shield us from the searing pain that rips through us after a tragedy, especially if we've lost someone close to us. A jagged hole has been torn in our hearts.

The anguish, this hemorrhage of the soul, seems unbearable and inescapable because of the unexpected and permanent loss of people and things we had come to know, love, and depend on. This agony is a cruel irony because there is a direct correlation between the depth of our anguish and the depth of our attachment to what we've lost. If we love deeply, we'll hurt deeply when we lose those we love. In *Bereavement: Studies of Grief in Adult Life,* C. M. Parkes writes, "The pain of grief is just as much a part of life as the joy of love; it is, perhaps, the price we pay for love, the cost of commitment" (pp. 5-6).

We writhe in pain when someone precious to us has been snatched from us. Then fear sets in—the fear of living in a world of risk, danger, and uncertainty.

Fear

Fear and panic descend on those who are desperately struggling to find solid footing after being rocked by a disaster. In this stage of vulnerability, people grapple with thoughts like:

- Am I going to make it through this?
- What am I going to do without him or her?
- Will I ever be able to work again?
- What am I going to tell my friends and family about this?
- How can I go on living without my best friend to share it with me?

- Will my life ever be normal again?
- Will I ever laugh again?
- Will I ever be able to forget what I've seen?

Whenever we go through a tragic disaster that wipes out life as we know it, the fear of not *surviving* becomes a primary preoccupation. Living without the security of precious loved ones and familiar surroundings seems not only impossible but unthinkable. And the dread that it could happen again —another fire, flood, tornado, earthquake, assault, attack, or accident—fuels our fears.

The unfairness of the situation leads us to anger.

Anger

"This can't be happening to me! It isn't fair! What did I do to deserve this?" are normal responses from people struggling to find meaning in the turmoil of a disaster.

Remember, anger over a tragic loss is to be expected. Plans and dreams have been shattered. The landscape of the future has been forever altered. What was once normal, expected, and often taken for granted is gone, wiped out in a few brief moments.

Normal is no longer *normal*. Everything has changed. And we don't like the changes. We want life back the way it was. And because we can't have it back, we get mad.

While all struggle and loss provoke anger at some level, tragedy intensifies the anger of those who survive. Whenever someone can be identified as the cause of the tragedy, the anger becomes much more complex. The demand for justice and revenge against those responsible for our pain and fear increases the normal level of anger that accompanies a painful loss.

Abandonment

Those left to pick up the pieces of their lives after a disaster often feel abandoned and alone. Their loved ones, their home, their town, their place of employment, their life as they knew it may have been wiped out. Now they feel the burden of going it alone.

For those who experience a disaster firsthand and live to tell about it, there is also a separateness that feels strange and unwanted. They may be the object of media attention they feel is undeserved. They're uncomfortable with the "hero" label. All they did was survive, while others who experienced the same disaster died.

Some of the anger in the initial stages of traumatic grief can also be attributed to a feeling of abandonment. This is especially true in the case of loved ones who left critical details undone before their deaths. Financial quagmires, insufficient insurance, no will, or no sound estate planning often add to the bereaved one's feelings of abandonment.

Isolation

When hit by a tragedy, we often feel alone and isolated by a silence that grips our hearts. We don't feel like talking because we think: *"No one could possibly understand what I'm going through. How* could they? They haven't walked in my shoes. They haven't seen what I've seen. They don't have a clue what I'm feeling. No one can fully understand my pain, loneliness, and fear!"

People often withdraw from friends and family who could be a valuable source of comfort in those crucial first stages of sorting through the rubble of a disaster. But often the sheer magnitude of the shock, pain, fear, and anger so overwhelms the survivor that a self-imposed form of exile somehow seems best.

Being Overwhelmed

A catastrophe hammers us with a barrage of feelings that just don't seem to quit. Like being in the ring with a heavyweight fighter who relentlessly pummels his opponent with his left jabs and sets him up for the crushing blow of his right hook, tragedy has a way of knocking us off balance and then slamming us to the mat. We're left reeling from the blows, emotionally battered and stunned.

An Inability To Focus

The cumulative effect of emotional overload is an inability to focus on basic necessities. Survivors, rescue workers, and those grieving the loss sometimes forget to eat, sleep, change their clothes, comb their hair, or take care of the basic needs of daily living. Normal functioning is labored at best and often feels impossible and futile. "Why bother? Everything is ruined anyway."

Tragedy: What It Takes From Us

Tragedies provoke a profound sense of disruption. All that we once thought safe, secure, and stable seems gone. Things we'd hoped for, dreamed about, and counted on have evaporated before our eyes. The course of life that we had charted for ourselves has been abruptly and radically diverted into harm's way. It's not merely a feeling that the wheels have fallen off but that they have been torn out from under us, and we are plummeting over a cliff.

We experience our vulnerability most acutely through the series of losses that follow in the wake of a tragedy.

Loss Of Safety

The world isn't a safe place. Most of us know that, but few of us live as if it's true. Instead, we tend to cultivate a level of self-delusion, convincing ourselves that we're really safe from harm. Tragedy exposes the undeniable reality of just how vulnerable we really are.

Herman Melville wrote about this lack of safety in his classic, *Moby Dick*: "All men live enveloped in whale-lines. All are born with halters round their necks; but it is only when caught in the swift, sudden turn of death, that mortals realize the silent, subtle, everpresent perils of life" (Penguin, p.387).

While sorrow, suffering, struggle, loss, and grief should be expected in a flawed and fallen world, most of us work exceptionally hard to avoid risk and ensure personal comfort. The gale-force winds of tragedy shred the gossamer veil of safety we've erected to deal with the daily anxieties of life.

Melville's words echo Jesus' warning to His closest followers. He didn't want them to be lulled into believing that living in this world would bring safety or security. On their last evening together, while assuring His disciples that He would not leave them alone, He said, "In this world you will have trouble" (Jn. 16:33).

The word Jesus used for "trouble" has to do with the pressure we feel in the midst of affliction, oppression, and intense distress. The apostle John would later use this same word to describe the worst time of "tribulation" that mankind will ever face (Rev. 7:14). It's a form of trouble that isn't merely annoying or distracting; it discourages, derails, and disables us when we get hit with it. Jesus knew that we would face many threats to our safety and security that would cause us to buckle under the pressure.

Tragedy exposes just how unsafe we really are, and it reminds us that we're not in control.

Loss Of Control
Tragedy can shatter the illusion of being in control in this dangerous world. If there's one thing the

events of September 11, 2001, have taught the world, it's that no one is ever really in control. Not only is this true of catastrophic events with widespread global impact, but it's also true of the millions of less publicized individual tragedies that occur every day.

The ominous power of a natural disaster—a typhoon, tornado, hurricane, flood, or earthquake—like few other events in our lives, forces us to face the unavoidable and stark reality that we have little if any control over the things and people that matter the most to us. No matter how deeply we love our family or friends, our love will not protect them from harm, pain, or death. The control we believed we once had quickly evaporates under the scorching heat of tragic circumstances. When we finally surrender to the truth that life is dangerous, death is sure, vulnerability is inescapable, and there is little we can do to make much of a difference, we find ourselves desperately needing answers for our lost confidence.

Loss Of Confidence

In his bestseller *Where Is God When It Hurts?* Philip Yancey writes, "Doubt follows pain quickly and surely, like a reflex action" (p. 77). Tragic disasters can dismantle our confidence that we can adequately deal with anything life throws at us. Although we may have confidently managed our lives in the past, tragedy forces us to question our ability to handle much of anything.

Victims of disasters, assaults, wars, or accidents are haunted by doubts and "what ifs." The details leading up to, during, and after a tragic event seem to replay endlessly: "What if I hadn't gone to work that day? What if I had? What if I had left early? What if I had gone in late?" A survivor relentlessly sorts through scenarios, hoping to find some overlooked shred of evidence that could have been used to avert the disaster. But when none is found, confidence disappears along with a loss of perspective.

Loss Of Perspective

People with little or no faith often find themselves faced with spiritual choices they had not considered before. At first, when things are clearly out of control and overwhelming, they tend to instinctively pray for help and intervention to a God they may not know. Then, after some distance from the shock of it all, they begin just as predictably to blame God or at least question His presence or absence in the tragedy.

Yancey writes, "Suffering calls our most basic beliefs about God into question" (p. 77). That's true for people of faith as well as those with only a casual acquaintance with God. Followers of Christ are invited by Him to believe that God is good and delights in giving good gifts to His children (Mt. 7:11; Lk. 11:13).

The undermining impact of a disaster, however, is that it can push us headlong into doubts about God and His goodness that we thought we'd settled long ago.

When we're squeezed by the vice-grip of tragedy, a core question erupts. Larry Crabb asks, "How do we trust a sometimes disappointing, seemingly fickle God who fails to do for us what good friends, if they could, would do?" (*Shattered Dreams*, p.34). After all, we assume, He's God, He's in charge, yet somehow He failed us.

The Bible tells about people of deep faith who battled with doubts about God after suffering tragic losses:

- Job demanded an audience with God to argue over the loss of his fortune, family, and health (Job 13:3–14:1).
- Asaph expressed his bitterness to God over His apparent indifference toward the prosperity of the wicked when compared to the suffering of the faithful (Ps. 73).
- Jeremiah voiced his complaint that his suffering was a direct result of God's deception (Jer. 20:7-18).
- John the Baptist expressed uncertainty about Jesus' identity as Messiah when under the duress of unjust imprisonment (Mt. 11:2).
- Even Jesus, when facing the darkest hour of His suffering, asked to be released from it (Mt. 26:39,42). And He felt abandoned by His Father when He took on the sins of the world (Mt. 27:46).

When confidence is lost and perspective is skewed by tragic events, despair sets in and steals hope.

Loss Of Hope

Tragedy hammers hope the hardest. And hope is what keeps us alive. Despair can set in when dreams are shattered (Prov. 13:12). The agony that life will never be the same again compels us to ask the question: "Why bother going on when what I deeply want is gone? When my spouse, my children, my health, my career, my home, my life are all gone, what's left to live for?"

Viktor Frankl, a survivor of the Nazi horrors of WWII, wrote, "Despair is suffering without meaning" (Yancey, p. 200). When we're overwhelmed by tragedy—our confidence shattered, our security threatened, and our perspective distorted—it's often impossible to see any meaning or positive outcome from our pain.

Initially, that's understandable. But facing life and facing loss isn't an event, it's a journey of the wounded to live again. Scarred, but still standing.

Tragedy: What It Leaves Behind

Tragedies not only take from us but they also leave us with scars we never wanted in the first place—such as survivor guilt, traumatic grief, and acute and post-traumatic stress disorders. Let's see how each of these scars affect survivors of tragedies.

Survivor Guilt

For those who live through a horrific disaster in which others around them are seriously injured or killed, they and their families often find it hard to celebrate their survival while others are grieving their losses.

Frequently, survivors are haunted by a gnawing sense of guilt about being alive. Instead of being grateful, they feel extremely ambivalent. "How dare I celebrate when others are grieving?" "Why did I live when so many around me died?" "Why didn't I do more to save the others?" This is especially true when their survival seems to have had more to do with coincidence than some conscious choice on their part.

Some have even gone so far as to adopt the irrational belief that somehow their survival was at the expense of others who were lost. Men can especially feel "cowardly" if in their attempts to save their own lives, they believe they may have harmed others.

This false guilt fuels an unhealthy sense of shame, inadequacy, and self-contempt that shatters a survivor's self-confidence.

For those who survive a tragedy, the joy of being alive can seem inconsistent with the sadness over those who died. Gratefulness for life can breed guilt. "How can I be happy when others died and their families are sad?" This dissonance complicates the rebuilding process for survivors, their families, and friends. And it often leads to traumatic grief.

Traumatic Grief

All tragedies imply loss. Losses of any kind provoke grief. Grief is the painful process of adjusting to life without the things and the people that we cherish in it (see the RBC Ministries Discovery Series booklet *How Can I Live With My Loss?* at www.rbc.org). But the shock wave of an unexpected and tragic loss catapults those left behind into an intensified level of grief known as traumatic grief.

Joanne Jozefowski writes, "Traumatic grief is a direct response to disastrous events that threaten our own safety, security, and beliefs around which we structure and order our lives" (*The Phoenix Phenomenon,* p. 230).

Those who lose a loved one, a home, or a community through traumatic circumstances are more likely to need professional help in dealing with their grief. The more violent, horrific, and unexpected the loss, the more complicated and prolonged the grief.

People who grieve well don't hurt less. Instead, they use their pain productively as an opportunity to *grow* through it rather than just *go* through it. And that process requires time.

Grief is not an event; it's a journey. Life will never be the same again, but it can be good again. Our journey through grief sometimes reveals things we never would have seen without it.

Jesus told a story about two houses built on different foundations (Mt. 7:24-27). Both houses were hit with the same torrential rainstorm that produced flash flooding and gale-force winds. One crumbled, but the other didn't. The one built on a foundation of solid rock endured the storm while the one built on sand was destroyed.

Tragedy has a way of exposing our foundations. No matter what the cause, how we weather the storms of life will ultimately depend on the foundation on which we've built our lives.

The Bible provides two foundational truths we can rely on while walking the path of traumatic grief:

- Tragic struggles and losses, no matter what the source, are often opportunities for growth (Rom. 5:3-5).
- Even in the middle of tragic struggles, God is present and able to do something good for us, no matter how much our circumstances may seem to indicate otherwise (Jer. 29:11; Rom. 8:28).

Some of the choices we make in the process of working through our grief can slowly bring meaning and hope back into our lives. No one chooses grief, but everyone eventually chooses how to respond to it.

For some, tragic events lead to complications that require special help. That's when the resources and training of professional counselors can be helpful.

Acute Stress Disorder (ASD)

Within a month of being exposed to a traumatic, life-threatening event that provoked feelings of intense fear, helplessness, or horror, some people experience difficulty adjusting to normal life. This readjustment period may last from 2 days to a month.

Some indicators that professional help may be needed to work through the aftermath of a trauma are the following:

- numbness, detachment, or absence of normal emotions
- reduction in awareness of one's surroundings, like "being in a daze"
- loss of interest in or participation in significant activities
- estrangement or detachment from others
- inability to recall important aspects of the trauma
- persistent reliving of the trauma through recurrent images, thoughts, dreams, illusions, or flashbacks

- avoidance of any potential reminder of the trauma
- anxiety or increased arousal indicated by difficulty sleeping, irritability, poor concentration, hypervigilance, exaggerated startle response, or motor restlessness.

Unfortunately, the media blitz covering tragic events amplifies our exposure to trauma well beyond the scope of those directly involved in them. Adults and children alike can be indirectly traumatized by the horrific images of violence, disaster, and accidents instantaneously broadcast into our homes 24/7 via the electronic media. This can result in symptoms of acute stress.

These symptoms impair our ability to function normally, causing significant distress in our relationships.

Post-Traumatic Stress Disorder (PTSD)

According to the National Center for PTSD, approximately 17 million people living in North America are exposed to trauma and disaster annually. Of those, about 25-30 percent develop chronic PTSD or other psychiatric disorders (*Disaster Mental Health Services: A Guidebook*, p. 2).

Most of us are aware of PTSD from the struggles American vets brought back from the horrors of the Vietnam War. PTSD is a prolonged adverse reaction to acute stress brought on by exposure to extremely traumatic events involving actual or threatened death, serious injury, torture, or confinement. The same basic symptoms for ASD apply to the diagnosis for PTSD.

In short, PTSD is ASD on steroids. It is a more protracted and intensified form of acute stress, lasting longer than a month, and if chronic, can plague a survivor for years. The onset of this disorder can be delayed for up to 6 months after the trauma—until something triggers the disturbing memories of the event.

PTSD causes significant disturbance, distress, or impairment in all areas of the survivor's life—socially, occupationally, relationally, and spiritually.

When distressful reactions begin to infiltrate and inhibit our daily functioning at home, school, or work, we need to take steps to seek help. That's when professional counselors trained in grief therapy and trauma for ASD or PTSD can help survivors and their families. A process of telling their story, appropriate grief, anxiety reduction, stress management, and ongoing support helps them live productive and healthy lives in spite of the painful memories of past traumas.

Tragedy: What It Can Teach Us

Most of us would prefer to avoid a tragedy. That's normal. But terror-management specialists argue that a confrontation with tragedy and death has "the potential to be a liberating and growth-enhancing experience." (*In the Wake of 9/11*, p. 139). Their conclusions agree with those of the ancient writer of Ecclesiastes. He recognized the value in facing tragedy and death:

> *It is better to go to a house of mourning than to go to a house of feasting, for death is the destiny of every man; the living should take this to heart (Eccl. 7:2).*

Tragedy, especially one through which we face our own mortality, often forces us to challenge untested beliefs about our purpose and significance in the world. Like no other event in life, it demands that we reevaluate how and why we live the way we do. Like it or not, deeply held convictions are most often strongly forged in the furnace of trauma and overwhelming adversity.

Learning through trauma is especially arduous because it demands much more than seeing reality clearly. It demands admitting and accepting reality at its ugliest. And it's often in the midst of that ugliness that we learn the most crucial lessons that form the foundations for the rest of our lives.

What Matters Most

Like sailors using the North Star to navigate and align their ship in the right direction, traumatic crises often force us to check our alignment to what matters most. We can be so easily distracted by the cares and concerns of daily living that we lose the larger perspective on what gives us meaning and purpose in this dangerous world.

In the final analysis, it all boils down to what we believe provides eternal meaning and significance in life. According to the Bible, it comes from our relationship with God and our relationship with others through Christ.

Knowing And Loving God. Jesus distilled all the writings of the Old Testament down to two fundamental commands that help us maintain a godly perspective on life, even when tragedy strikes. The first is found in Matthew 22:37-38.

> *"Love the Lord your God with all your heart and with all your soul and with all your mind." This is the first and greatest commandment.*

Loving God is the fundamental relationship around which all others must align. This is not optional. It is essential. If any other relationship, no matter how important it is, assumes God's primary position of being our North Star, every other relationship will be doomed to failure. We can make it our goal to trust and to please Him (2 Cor. 5:9,15). Otherwise, nothing else really matters.

Once our relationship with God is set in place, we are free to reorient the remainder of our relationships around Him.

Loving Others. Jesus completed His thought in verses 39-40:

> *The second is like it: "Love your neighbor as yourself." All of the Law and the Prophets hang on these two commandments.*

Who is most precious to us? Our spouse? Our children? Our parents? Our friends? All other relationships are most fully enhanced by our love for God that overflows into our love for others. In fact, genuine love for others is our deepest expression of obedient love for God (Rom. 12:9; 1 Pet. 4:8-11; 1 Jn. 3:11-18).

What Doesn't Matter Much At All

Tragedy teaches us to trivialize the trivial. In spite of what popular culture tells us, what *doesn't* matter much at all in the final analysis is our agenda and our stuff.

Our Agenda. What do we cherish the most? Often, what gets exposed in times of tragic loss is the fact that we are devoted to running our lives according to our agenda rather than God's. We often pray for Him to cooperate with our plans to fulfill our dreams rather than humbly submitting our hearts to follow His call.

When tragedy unexpectedly interrupts, our agenda is clearly seen for what it really is—our foolish plans.

Our Stuff. What we also discover, much to our chagrin, is how much time and energy we waste majoring on the minors and minoring on the majors. Our priorities are often out of whack. We may pay lip service to the importance of loving God and loving others, yet we invest most of our time, talents, and resources building our net worth, planning our next vacation, and saving for retirement. While these are good things, our passion to see people grow in Christ gets lost in the scramble to get ahead.

Painful clarity comes in times of tragic upheaval. In the good times when we are satisfied with how well things are going, we tend to forget the Lord, just as Israel did after entering the Promised Land (Dt. 6:10-12). God desires our heartfelt devotion in times of triumph as well as tragedy. Unfortunately, He often needs to use tragic events to get our attention.

If we allow God to teach us through our tragedies, then He can equip us to live more confidently in a dangerous world.

Living Confidently In A Dangerous World

In his book *The Survivor Personality*, Al Siebert writes, "People seldom tap into their deepest strengths and abilities until forced to do so by a major adversity" (p. 7).

Writing almost 70 years earlier, Virginia Woolf would have agreed: "Life . . . is arduous, difficult, a perpetual struggle. It calls for gigantic courage and strength. . . . Creatures of illusion as we are, it calls for confidence in oneself. Without self-confidence we are as babes in the cradle" (*A Room of One's Own*, pp. 34-35).

These sobering words of vulnerability are laced with encouragement. They aren't sappy sentiment but reflect a firm grip on reality entwined with hope, like Jesus' final words to His disciples on their last night together. Before He prayed for them and then went to the cross, Jesus taught them:

> *I have told you these things, so that in Me you may have peace. In this world you will have trouble. But take heart! I have overcome the world (Jn. 16:33).*

These words were both a sober warning and an encouragement to the disciples, who would soon be facing extreme persecution and trauma. Although they had no clue what the next few hours, days, or years would hold, Jesus was preparing them for what was ahead. He knew His death would dismantle them. He knew they would be oppressed, afflicted, distressed, and pressured from all sides. Trouble would be the norm. But He didn't leave them there alone.

He offered them hope. What He shared with them was to bring them peace in the midst of their run through the troubling gauntlet of life. Paul, a later disciple, would describe this peace as transcending all understanding while guarding their hearts and minds in Christ (Phil. 4:7).

Peace in the midst of tumultuous trouble was Jesus' encouragement—a new kind of normal. Courage to remain faithful was His command. And a Comforter to be their constant inner source of strength was His provision (Jn. 16:7-14).

After He taught them, Jesus led the way through the gauntlet of agony, grief, and suffering ahead of them and us. He paved the way for us to overcome in a dangerous world of tragedy and trouble.

Run The Gauntlet Well

Athletes who excel in any sport have to face injury and pain. The same is true of those who have run through the gauntlet of life. Tragedies leave us scarred. No one gets through unscathed. We all live with scars of the traumatic battles we've endured. And though we may walk with a limp as evidence that we've paid the price and run the race, we can walk with confidence because our hope in God has been strengthened through adversity.

Survivors who have grown through tragedy are more humble and hopeful because of what they have endured. And they can truly sing with the psalmist:

God is our refuge and strength, an ever-present help in trouble. Therefore we will not fear . . . . The Lord Almighty is with us (Ps. 46:1-2, 7).

Remember, we can use the painful resistance of tragedy to strengthen our faith for the path ahead.

Focus On What You Still Have

People who mature through tragedy have learned and now believe that trauma, disaster, and even death will never have the final word. They still grieve over what they've lost, but their grieving, as well as their living, is entwined with hope (1 Th. 4:13) because they focus on what they still have and can never lose.

These hopeful survivors not only honor those they have lost but they also live to love and enjoy those they still have. With Christ as our hope in times of tragedy, all is never lost.

We have a tendency, however, to lose focus when we encounter trouble. The writer of Hebrews reminds us that when adversity distracts us from our focus on Christ, we will grow weary and lose heart (12:2-3).

This pattern of losing focus is especially prevalent after a catastrophic disaster. We must be careful not to lose our focus on Christ. When we keep our eyes on Him, we will be able to sing with the psalmist in Psalm 119:71, "It was good for me to be afflicted so that I might learn Your decrees."

While much in life can hurt us deeply, no tragedy, not even death, can steal our hope in Christ or separate us from His love (Rom. 8:35-39).

Honor Those You've Lost

Many people honor their loved ones by using their memory as a springboard to do something positive that gives encouragement to those still living.

In memory of her husband Todd, Lisa Beamer started a foundation to help kids who lost parents in the attacks of 9/11. She also wrote a book about her journey through traumatic grief. She accepts invitations to share her story and to encourage others in their tragedy. It wasn't a platform she wanted, but it is a platform she's been willing to use to redeem a tragic loss that at one point seemed unredeemable.

Connect With Other Survivors

One of the most successful ways that survivors of trauma are helped is to be connected with others who share similar experiences.

Survivors need to talk. They need to tell their stories. They need to know that someone listening truly understands their invisible wounds—the horror, terror, isolation, guilt, loneliness, rage, and grief that they bear.

They also need to listen. They need to hear other survivors talk about their struggles to make sense out of a senseless event. They need hope to be able to live well in spite of their scars.

How To Help

People experience trauma in varying degrees. There are the primary survivors who have lived through the epicenter of the trauma. There are the families of survivors. There are the grieving families of victims who died. There are the families who survived but lost everything. Recognize that you are not called to help everyone, but you may be able to help someone. While some help does require specialized training, a willingness to be used of God to "carry each other's burdens" (Gal. 6:2) is what's needed.

Consider how to help the tragedy-stricken:

Give Them Time

Do not require anything from a survivor or family member of a survivor, especially in the initial stages. Give them time and space to grieve. Allow them to process their hurt while you try to see, hear, and feel their pain with them. Let them know that it is okay to feel whatever they are feeling. This is crucial to their journey through the traumatic valley of pain.

Don't Try To Fix It

Nothing you do can fix the problem. You can't change history, raise the dead, or restore what's been lost.

Just sitting with those who are in pain can be encouraging to them. Not having anything to say is okay. Nothing will eliminate the pain, but a touch or a hug reassures them of your presence and gives them a taste of the presence of the God of hope in you (Col. 1:27). Your presence has power.

Weep With Them

One of the most precious gifts we can offer to people who have tragically lost loved ones is the gift of our tears. We need to listen to them share their pain, to share their tears, to grieve with them over what they have lost, and to rejoice with them over what they still have (Rom. 12:15).

Meet Immediate Needs

People in the initial stages of trauma are so distraught by the pain that they often forget to take care of themselves. Decisions that previously would have been almost second nature are now totally forgotten.

Assisting those in grief with funeral arrangements, sorting through paperwork, choosing clothes for the funeral, transporting family members, ironing clothes for the funeral, and many other immediate needs can help keep them from feeling so alone.

Pray With Them And For Them

In some of the stages of trauma, people often find they just can't pray. Interceding on behalf of the brokenhearted is a privilege we dare not overlook. Imagine the encouragement we bring to those who feel too exhausted to pray when they hear us bring their name to the throne of God.

Our Ultimate Refuge
& Hope

Where do we find unshakable confidence to go on when tragedy strikes? King David, a man familiar with tragedy throughout his life, wrote, "Find rest, O my soul, in God alone; my hope comes from Him. He alone is my rock and my salvation; He is my fortress, I will not be shaken. My salvation and my honor depend on God; He is my mighty rock, my refuge. Trust in Him at all times" (Ps. 62:5-8). David's exhortation 3,000 years ago is still true today.

The only refuge for the battered and broken-hearted is a relationship with the God who has shown how deeply He loves and cares for us (Rom. 5:8).

Jesus invites us to a life of confidence, even when faced with loss. He said, "Do not let your hearts be troubled. Trust in God; trust also in Me" (Jn. 14:1).

Trusting in Jesus means depending on Him for what can never be lost (Jn. 1:12; 3:16; 10:10). His resurrection assures those who trust Him that they will receive His grace, mercy, peace, forgiveness, eternal life, and unfailing love (Rom. 8:31-39).

No matter what we may lose in this life, Jesus' assurance of His presence now and His promise of an eternal home in heaven can become our unshakable fortress of hope and peace in times of trouble.